"Succinct, clear, biblical and anthropological, Arbuckle confronts head-on conspiracy thinking and its concurrent Christian fundamentalism. He provides a set of tools, social, and evangelical, as an antidote to the current crisis of knowledge in which fake news and conspiratorial thinking cloud truth and destroy communities."
Professor Gerard Moore, Principal BBI-The Australian Institute of Theological Education

"An essential work for our time, this concise volume illumes the detrimental impact of conspiracy theories and their penchant to cause cultural chaos, fundamental biases, and scapegoating that denigrates not just individuals and religions but entire ethnic groups and countries. This book by an internationally acclaimed cultural anthropologist is a work of common sense and contextual theology, one that assists us all to better read 'the signs of the times'. A fascinating read, it will be of use to numerous academic disciplines and resonate with all people of goodwill."
Professor Anthony Maher, Australian Centre for Christianity and Culture

"I am amazed that such a small book can pack such a big punch in helping us understand where conspiracy theories come from, why they remain so persistent in light of scientific evidence to the contrary, and why they have such harmful consequences. In this global era of rapid social and cultural change, where people are desperate to make sense out of their lives, it couldn't be truer that Arbuckle's insights and clear explanations are for such a time as this. He brings to this book the rare combination of a cultural anthropologist and Scripture scholar to address the problems of conspiracy theorizing, but he doesn't leave us there, he reminds us that faith in Christ is greater than the evil that can sometimes preoccupy us."
Darrell Whiteman, author of *Crossing Cultures with the Gospel: Anthropological Wisdom for Effective Christian Witness.*

Conspiracy Theorizing

Conspiracy Theorizing explores how individuals with the Christian faith should react to conspiracy theories, their untruths, and their dangers. This book outlines the way that conspiracy theories are the fundamental basis for stigmatization and scapegoating. It goes further to explain that scapegoating fosters extreme divisions within societies and between nations, with each side often demonizing the other.

This book describes how conspiracy theories satisfy people's needs for certainty, security, and a positive self-image in a world that they feel is disintegrating. When the comforting securities of cultures crumble, paranoia makes sense. This book demonstrates that an inability to live with uncertainty and ambiguity draws people to conspiracy theories when they confirm their apprehensions. It also shows that, since conspiracy theories can never be verified by objective research and truths, they are one of the most difficult subjects to uncover.

This book aims to answer these questions: What are conspiracy theories? Why do they arise, especially in times of cultural upheavals? Are they harmful? Are conspiracy theories a type of magical thinking? What do the Christian Scriptures say about them? Readers interested in religion, Christianity, and conspiracy theories would enjoy this book.

Gerald A. Arbuckle, SM, theologian and Cambridge-trained social anthropologist, is an award-winning author; his most recent book is *The Pandemic and the People of God*. He was recently awarded an honorary Doctorate of the Australian Catholic University 'for bringing the interplay between faith and reason to bear on complex religious and social policy issues.'

Routledge Focus on Religion

Theology and Climate Change
Paul Tyson

Religion and Euroscepticism in Brexit Britain
Ekaterina Kolpinskaya and Stuart Fox

Owning the Secular
Religious Symbols, Culture Wars, Western Fragility
Matt Sheedy

Cross-Cultural and Religious Critiques of Informed Consent
Edited by Joseph Tham, Alberto García Gómez, and Mirko Daniel Garasic

Worldview Religious Studies
Douglas J Davies

White Evangelicals and Right-Wing Populism
How Did We Get Here?
Marcia Pally

Rape Culture in the House of David
A Company of Men
Barbara Thiede

Counseling Survivors of Religious Abuse
Paula J. Swindle, Craig C. Cashwell, and Jodi L. Tangen

Conspiracy Theorizing
Analysis and Scriptural Critique
Gerald A. Arbuckle

For more information about this series, please visit: www.routledge.com/Routledge-Focus-on-Religion/book-series/RFR

Conspiracy Theorizing
Analysis and Scriptural Critique

Gerald A. Arbuckle

LONDON AND NEW YORK

First published 2024
by Routledge
4 Park Square, Milton Park, Abingdon, Oxon OX14 4RN

and by Routledge
605 Third Avenue, New York, NY 10158

Routledge is an imprint of the Taylor & Francis Group, an informa business

© 2024 Gerald A. Arbuckle

The right of Gerald A. Arbuckle to be identified as authors of this work has been asserted in accordance with sections 77 and 78 of the Copyright, Designs and Patents Act 1988.

All rights reserved. No part of this book may be reprinted or reproduced or utilised in any form or by any electronic, mechanical, or other means, now known or hereafter invented, including photocopying and recording, or in any information storage or retrieval system, without permission in writing from the publishers.

Trademark notice: Product or corporate names may be trademarks or registered trademarks, and are used only for identification and explanation without intent to infringe.

British Library Cataloguing-in-Publication Data
A catalogue record for this book is available from the British Library

ISBN: 978-1-032-75048-4 (hbk)
ISBN: 978-1-032-75052-1 (pbk)
ISBN: 978-1-003-47216-2 (ebk)

DOI: 10.4324/9781003472162

Typeset in Times New Roman
by Apex CoVantage, LLC

For Vincent Long Van Nguyen, OFM Conv, DD.

Contents

Acknowledgements   xi
Overview of the book   xii

Introduction   1

1   Gossip: The Breeding Ground of Conspiracy Theorizing   7

Defining Gossip 8
Gossip and Violence 12
Gossip and Power 14
Gossips Shame 17
Gossip and Cultural Upheaval 19
Scriptural Critique 21
Summary Points 25
Discussion Questions 25

2   Conspiracy Theorizing Uncovered   31

Conspiracy Theory: Definitions 33
Types of Conspiracy Theories 34
Why Do Conspiracy Theories Flourish? 40
Conspiracy Theories Cause Harm 42
Responding to Conspiracy Theories 44
Scriptural Critique 45
Summary Points 48
Discussion Questions 48

3 Conspiracy Theorizing Drives Scapegoating, Populism and Polarization   55

Defining Scapegoating 56
Origins of Scapegoating 57
Ethnocentrism: Theories of Origins 58
Cultural Trauma: Scapegoating and Polarization
   Intensify 63
Pre-Covid-19 64
Covid-19: Democracies Threatened 65
Scriptural Critique 73
Summary Points 76
Discussion Questions 76

4 Conspiracy Theorizing and Magical Thinking: Is There a Connection?   86

Magical Thinking and Action Explained 87
Magic and Conspiracy Thinking in Premodernity 93
Magic and Conspiracy Thinking in Postmodernity 97
Scriptural Critique 104
Summary Points 107
Discussion Questions 108

Conclusion   110

Index   *120*

Acknowledgements

My particular thanks to Dr Thomas Ryan, SM, and Professor Gerard Moore, who patiently read the text and offered astute comments; members of the community at Campion Hall, Oxford University, where the primary research for this book took place. These people, however, are in no way responsible for any shortcomings of the book. My gratitude also to the following editors for permission to quote and adapt material I have originally published: Dr Gerard Kelly, "From Gossip to Conspiracy Thinking: Analysis and Scriptural Evaluations," in the *Australian Catholic Record*, vol. 99, no. 2 (2022): 187–200; Ms Betsy Crosby, "Retelling 'The Good Samaritan'" in *Journal of the Catholic Health Association of the United States*, July-August 2007, 20–24; and Mr Hans Christoffersen, Liturgical Press, in *Violence, Society, and the Church: A Cultural Approach* (2004): 80–83, 86–87, 126–41, and in *Fundamentalism at Home and Abroad: Analysis and Pastoral Responses* (2017): xii-xiii, 44–45, 76.

Overview of the Book[1]

This is a book of academic practical theology as seen through the lenses particularly of cultural anthropology and the Christian scriptures. Why turn to cultural anthropology? Culture gives us a sense of belonging. When a culture suddenly disintegrates for whatever reason, we feel lost in the chaos and prone to unhealthy remedies, such as conspiracy theories, to regain the feeling of belonging. Culture matters! So anthropology is about how people feel and communicate within and across cultures. It is often about revealing the cultural forces that motivate people and their institutions, although they are commonly unaware of the existence of these forces and their ability to affect behaviour. As we will see, this is so often the case with devotees of conspiracy theories. Anthropologists delve beneath the surface of social life to uncover its underlying dynamics, asking questions that disturb traditional cultural ways of thinking. This particular academic discipline has been called by Raymond Firth "an inquisitive, challenging, uncomfortable discipline . . . if not destroying fictions and empty phrases . . . at least exposing them."[2]

Each chapter ends with relevant scriptural critique and discussion questions. All four Gospels are narratives about the person of Christ; the focus is on the experience of Christ, the revelation of God. The more the early Christians contemplated the story of Jesus in light of their own particular social, political, and economic circumstances, the more they could believe in Christ's loving concern for them as individuals and communities. In repeating his parables and rereading what he said and did, they discovered the values and narratives that should shape their lives. It was not an abstract or academic knowledge of Christ but a belief in a person who intimately cared for, and loved, them. To know Christ was for them "a dynamic, experiential, relational activity involving the whole person and finding expression in a lived response of loving obedience to God's will."[3]

This scriptural pedagogical method of "see, judge, act" is followed in this book. The reader, after reading the first descriptive section of each

Overview of the Book xiii

chapter, is invited to then ponder the scriptural texts that follow asking themselves questions such as:

- What feelings do the scriptural passage evoke in me?
- What values in the scriptural text are especially relevant to shaping my reactions to the conspiracy theories?
- Does the scriptural passage inspire courage in me to do something, however small, to assist others to understand the challenges and dangers of conspiracy theories? Each chapter will conclude with further questions that focus on the material presented there.

Chapter 1: Gossip: The Breeding Ground of Conspiracy Theorizing

The private world of gossip provides a fertile ground for the beginning of conspiracy theorizing. Gossip is an act of violence that is designed to ruin an individual's or a group's reputation. It gratifies the envious and revengeful feelings gossips feel towards others by denigrating and scapegoating the victim's achievements; it provides gossips with a temporary sense of power over people and a feeling of bonding with their listeners. The scriptures contain many examples of gossip and its malevolent consequences. For example, Christ himself was frequently the object of gossip through whispering shaming campaigns. Gossip is condemned in both the Old Testament and the New Testament.

Chapter 2: Conspiracy Theorizing Uncovered

When the private world of gossip moves into the public arena, we have conspiracy theorizing and its malevolent qualities. True, such theorizing has been around for centuries. However, with the rapid spread of internet technology, there is now a tsunami of conspiracy theories of all kinds. Conspiracy theories flourish at times of cultural, economic, and political chaos. They are unverifiable truths. Since people *believe* conspiracy theories, it is usually impossible to undermine them with objective factual information. The scriptures call followers to be truthful people and not to be seduced by untruths at the heart of conspiracy theories. They are to be truth-tellers in imitation of Christ who is "the way, the truth, and the life" (John 14:6).

Chapter 3: Conspiracy Theorizing Drives Scapegoating, Populism, and Polarization

Conspiracy theorizing drives scapegoating. Scapegoating formally transforms malevolent judgements of others from a world of shared secrets in gossip directly into the public arena. By passing the blame for their afflictions on to others, people are able conveniently to distract themselves and others from the real causes and the efforts they must make to remove them. Scapegoating creates more and more extreme divisions in societies. The middle ground weakens. Populists dominate the media by embodying grievance and shaping or supporting existing conspiracy theories; when a conspiracy theory is debunked, they formulate another one. The Good Samaritan parable highlights the universal truths and values of solidarity, compassion, and justice that must infuse all decision-making and behaviour. The parable's mandate is not just about charity but charity accompanied by political, structural, and systemic conversion founded on justice.

Chapter 4: Conspiracy Theorizing and Magical Thinking: Is There a Connection?

This chapter explains that conspiracy theorizing and magical thinking can be connected or can overlap. There are two different ways of thinking: through either *mythos* (i.e. myths or mythology) or *logos* (i.e. rational, reality-based information). Magical thinking and conspiracy theories belong to *mythos*. A myth is a story or tradition that claims to reveal in an imaginative way a fundamental *belief* or *truth* about the world and human life. This truth is regarded as authoritative by those who believe it. On the other hand, authority for *logos* is not belief but what is proven to be externally and scientifically factual. The chapter gives examples of conspiracy theorizing and magical thinking in premodern and modern societies. The magical qualities of conspiracy theories in modern societies may be overt, or, unlike their counterparts in premodern cultures, they are more commonly covert. The Bible never states that magic such as sorcery or witchcraft is fake but affirms that it is helpless against the power of God. Magical thinking and actions are ultimate evils because they dare to substitute God with demons.

Notes

1 The themes of this book were first developed in a brief article by the author: "From Gossip to Conspiracy Thinking: Analysis and Scriptural Evaluation," *Australasian Catholic Record*, vol. 99, no. 2 (2022): 187–300.
2 Raymond Firth, "Engagement and Detachment: Reflections on Applying Social Anthropology to Social Affairs," *Human Organization*, no. 40 (1981): 200.
3 Thomas H. Groome, *Christian Religious Education: Sharing Our Story and Vision* (Melbourne: Dove, 1980), 144.

Introduction

> This is, in short, a golden age of conspiracy theories. . . . Their ability to motivate people is what makes them dangerous.
>
> *(The Economist)*[1]

> Conspiracy theories seem to fulfil a human need of making sense of an otherwise chaotic existence.
>
> (Eirikur Bergmann)[2]

The world is awash with conspiracy theories. They are the beliefs, contrary to reality, that individuals or groups are secretly acting to accomplish some malevolent purpose. Online platforms have only intensified the rapid global spread of such theories.

Once Covid-19 was identified, conspiracy theories emerged in a rush. Some said it was a hoax or a campaign to disrupt the presidential re-election of Donald Trump, while others stated the pharmaceutical industry spreads the disease. In New Zealand, in 2020, in an anti-lockdown rally attended by thousands, flags of people depicting the global conspiracy QAnon were clearly displayed.[3] In Australia there are people still opposed to Covid-19 vaccinations who claim that a global cabal is plotting to remove ordinary citizens' freedoms.[4] In 2022, three people in Queensland were gunned down by three terrorists motivated by the fundamentalist conspiracy theory of Christian premillennialism. Conspiracy theories have moved from the fringes of societies to the top levels of governments.[5] Even established democracies are not escaping the dangers of this social disease.[6]

Conspiracy theories satisfy people's needs for certainty, security, and a positive self-image in a world that they feel is disintegrating. When the comforting securities of cultures crumble, paranoia makes sense. An inability to live with uncertainty and ambiguity draws people to conspiracy theories when they validate their apprehensions. One story answers all their fears. Unfortunately since conspiracy theories can never be verified

DOI: 10.4324/9781003472162-1

by objective research and truths, they are one of the most problematic subjects to expose.

This small book of practical and contextual theology[7] aims to answer these questions: What are conspiracy theories? Why do they arise, especially in times of cultural upheavals? Are they harmful? What do the scriptures say about them? What pastoral advice can we offer believers of conspiracy theories?

This academic manuscript is a cultural anthropological and theological text. Hence, it is particularly directed at readers who are interested in these subjects and their relevance for understanding conspiracy theorizing.

Gossip and Conspiracy Theorizing

Conspiracy theories in the public arena begin in the private world of gossip. Gossip is the breeding ground for most conspiracy theories which are frequently rejuvenated and changed in a murky atmosphere. The dynamic of gossiping is mirrored in the public behaviour of conspiracy theorists who feed on a diet of gossip and use gossip to spread their falsehoods. Therefore, to better understand the world of conspiracy theorizing, we need to know how the fetid and secretive world of gossip operates and impacts its prey (see Chapter 1).

Gossip is one of the most powerful yet complex forms of human communication. A characteristic of all cultures, gossip is designed to ruin an individual's or a group's reputation. It is an avenue for the betrayal of secrets. It is "distilled malice."[8] Gossip gratifies the envy gossips feel towards others by denigrating their achievements; it provides gossips with a sense of power over people and a temporary feeling of bonding with their listeners.

Harmful Consequences

As with gossip, conspiracy stories are concerned about the struggle between good and evil, the battle between wicked people secretly acting to control the unwary masses and the minority who, having seen through their plot, are doing their upmost to prevent it.[9] Tragically conspiracy theories can cause immense harm to people, influencing political policy decisions and social behaviours. The theories are often associated with ideological extremism of any form, and throughout history significant political, economic, and cultural crises have encouraged highly divisive conspiracy theories to emerge.[10]

Today anti-vaccine conspiracy theories are still globally poisoning the minds and endangering the bodies of many citizens. Worse still, wars are fought and people are murdered as a consequence of these theories. Timothy McVeigh, the convicted bomber of the Oklahoma City federal building, firmly believed that the government was conspiring to undermine people's liberty.[11] A terrorist in New Zealand massacred forty-nine people in 2019 because he believed the conspiracy theory that Muslims were out to take over the country and the world (see Chapter 2).

Today scapegoating is fostering extreme divisions within societies and between nations, with each side often demonizing the other. In this situation populist authoritarian political leaders, such as Vladimir Putin and Donald Trump, emerge, whose abuse of power is initiated and bolstered by conspiracy theories. As Voltaire said in 1765, "Those who make you believe absurdities can make you commit atrocities." Conspiracy theories are the fundamental basis for this stigmatization and scapegoating.[12] If you want to provoke people to action, give them an "other" to target.[13]

By transferring the blame for their afflictions on others, people are able to distract themselves from the real causes of crises. To those who are losing ground politically, economically, or socially, these theories give them someone to blame.[14] Their leaders take advantage of this. Hitler claimed that the Jews were poisoning the German Aryan blood and Aryan soul, thus holding back Germany from becoming a dominant nation. Many Germans accepted this conspiracy theory. Tragically once people are dehumanized by a conspiracy theory there is nothing that cannot be done to them. The same pattern of abuse is happening today in Ukraine. Many Russians now believe the conspiracy theory that Russia is a besieged fortress encircled by Neo-Nazis Ukrainians, backed up by the West, and bent on destroying the fatherland. The result? Putin's campaign is to bomb Ukraine into powerlessness with the killing of thousands and thousands of innocent people (see Chapter 3).

Magical Thinking

Among academics there is an increasing interest in the connection between magical thinking and conspiracy theorizing. This is the first book written for the general reader to explain the link between the two types of thinking. The world of magic is a collection of beliefs that have no foundation in established experimental sciences and associated disciplines. Michael Barkun, an authority on conspiracy thinking, writes: "It should be no surprise that occultism and conspiracy theories have connections and overlaps. Both, after all, deal with knowledge that believers think has been concealed and which they alone understand."[15]

As this book explains, there are two *complementary* ways of thinking, speaking, and obtaining knowledge: through *mythos* (i.e. myth/mythology) and *logos* (reality-tested information).[16] Magical thinking and conspiracy theorizing belong to *mythos*. Both give meaning to believers in a world of threatening chaos.[17] Magic and conspiracy theorizing can interact for two reasons: they demand belief from their devotees since both claim to reveal truths that are rationally unverifiable, and both assume there are shadowy manipulators plotting behind the scenes (see Chapter 4).

Scriptural Critique

The potential for conspiracy theorizing is within every human heart and the evil of scapegoating is an inherent quality of this behaviour. Scapegoating falsely focuses on an external cause of problems, thus negating or lessening the guilt of the agent. It also makes people feel bonded as they unite with others to scapegoat the victims. Just as Adam, in the Genesis myth, tries to blame Eve for what has happened rather than admit his own role in the incident, every person has the capacity to blame others for their afflictions and to ignore their own role in causing them. Yet the commandment "Neither shall you bear false witness against your neighbor" (Deut 5:20) applies to all forms of scapegoating.

The Bible never states that the magical thinking in conspiracy theorizing is a fake but affirms that it is helpless against the power of God.[18] God sees magical thinking, and therefore conspiracy theorizing, as the ultimate evil because it dares to substitute God with demons. This is why the language against magic in all its forms is so vigorously uncompromising.

In order to resist the temptations of falling for conspiracy theorizing and magical thinking, Christians require faith and the practice of good works: "By faith we understand that the worlds were prepared by the word of God, so that what is seen was made from things that are not visible" (Heb 11: 3). Faith in the person of Jesus Christ and his mission alone must guide all our thoughts and actions: "let us run with perseverance the race that is set before us, looking to Jesus the pioneer and perfecter of our faith, who for the sake of the joy that was set before him endured the cross, disregarding its shame" (Heb 12:1-2). Earlier the writer in Psalm 119 offers comforting advice.[19] He feels he will be overwhelmed by the "false ways" (v.29), "vanity" (v.37), "lies" (v.37), and "arrogance" (vv.51, 69, 78, 85) of gossips and their conspiracy theories threatening him from every side, but he will remain faithful with God's help. He says: "The arrogant smear me with lies, but with my whole heart I will keep [God's] precepts . . . Uphold me according to your promise, that I may live, and let me not be put to shame in my hope" (Ps 119:69,116).

Notes

1 "From Congo to the Capitol, Conspiracy Theories Are Surging: Covid and the Internet Are Fuelling a Global Boom in Bonkers Beliefs," *The Economist* (September 3, 2021), 11.

2 Eirikur Bergmann, *Conspiracy and Populism: The Politics of Misinformation* (Oxford: Palgrave, 2018), 168.
3 See Jamie Morton, "Study Out of Politics of New Zealand Conspiracy Theorists," www.nzherald.co.nz/nz/study-on-politics-of-new-zealamd-conspiracy-theoristts/QWT30CABA6A2FLRF0FSWZDPT6QYA/ (Accessed June 27, 2022).
4 See Emily Baker, "Anti-Vax Group My Place Is Pushing to Take Control of Council Decisions," www.abc.net.au/news/2023-04-04/anti-vax-group-my-place-plan-to-influuence-your-local-council/102166182 (Accessed April 3, 2023).
5 Pope Francis even warned bishops before the Synod on Family, 2015, not to get caught up in "The Hermeneutic of Conspiracy," www.theguardian.com/world/2015/oct/08/pope-francis-warns-bisops-against-theories-ahead-of-the-synod (Accessed March 3, 2023).
6 See Martin Wolf, *The Crisis of Democratic Capitalism* (New York: Penguin Press, 2023), 370–82; Gerald A. Arbuckle, *The Pandemic and the People of God: Cultural Impacts and Pastoral Responses* (Maryknoll, NY: Orbis Books, 2021), xv–xxi, 87–109.
7 Pope Francis emphasizes that Catholic theology must become a fundamentally contextual theology, that is, a theology that engages with contemporary culture and people's lived experience, not a "desk-bound theology." See Apostolic Letter *Ad Theologiam Promovendum* (Vatican, November, 2023).
8 Christopher M. Elias, *Gossip Men* (Chicago: Chicago University Press, 2017), 13.
9 See Michael Butter, *The Nature of Conspiracy Theories* (Cambridge, UK: Polity Press, 2020), 32.
10 See Rob Brotherton, *Suspicious Minds: Why We Believe Conspiracy Theories* (New York: Bloomsbury Sigma, 2015); Susan Bell, "What Today's Conspiracy Theories Have in Common With Ancient Ones," (March 18, 2021) (PDF).
11 See R. Scott Appleby, *The Ambivalence of the Sacred: Religion, Violence, and Reconciliation* (Oxford: Rowman and Littlefield, 1993), 167–8.
12 See Michael Barkun, *A Culture of Conspiracy: Apocalyptic Visions in Contemporary America* (Berkeley, CA: University of California Press, 2013), 27.
13 See Barbara F. Walter, *How Civil Wars Start and How to Stop Them* (London: Viking, 2022), 215.
14 See Evan Osnos, *Wildland: The Making of America's Fury* (New York: Farrar, Straus and Giroux, 2021); Farah Stockman, *America Made: What Happens to People When Work Disappears* (New York: Random House, 2021); and Spencer Ackerman, *Reign of Terror: How the 9/11 Era Destabilized America and Produced Trump* (New York: Viking, 2021).
15 Michael Barkun, "Conspiracy Theories and the Occult," ed. Christopher Partridge, *The Occult World* (London: Routledge, 2016), 701.
16 See Karen Armstrong, *Sacred Nature: How We Recover Our Bond With the Natural World* (London: The Bodley Head, 2022), 21–30;

Gerald A. Arbuckle, *Fundamentalism at Home and Abroad: Analysis and Pastoral Responses* (Collegeville, MN: Liturgical Press, 2017), 31–2.

17 See David S. Katz, *The Occult Tradition: From the Renaissance to the Present Day* (London: Pimlico, 2007), 1–2.

18 See John L. McKenzie, *Dictionary of the Bible* (London: Geoffrey Chapman, 1965), 536.

19 See Walter Brueggemann and William H. Bellinger, Jr., *Psalms* (Cambridge: Cambridge University Press, 2014), 519–21.

1 Gossip
The Breeding Ground of Conspiracy Theorizing

A gossip goes about telling secrets, but the one who is trustworthy in spirit keeps a confidence.

(Prov 11:13)[1]

Full of envy, murder, strife, deceit, craftiness, they are gossips . . . inventors of evil.

(Rom 1:29)

Besides . . . they are . . . gossips and busybodies, saying what they should not say.

(1 Tim 5:13)

This chapter explains that:

- Gossip breeds, rejuvenates, and spreads conspiracy theories.
- Gossip aims to destroy reputations.
- Gossip binds people together in a fragile way.
- Gossip flourishes in turbulent times.
- The Scriptures condemn gossip.

This chapter focuses on gossip as the breeding ground and spreader of conspiracy theories. Conspiracy theories in the public arena begin in the private world of gossip and are frequently rejuvenated and changed in its shadowy atmosphere. The behaviour of conspiracy devotees mirrors that of gossipers; they will publicly control, bully, shame, and scapegoat the innocent just as gossips privately do to their victims.

So, to better understand how in the public arena malevolent conspiracy theorizing operates and its impact on its victims, we need to be alert first to the secretive world of gossipers.

Gossip is one of the most formidable yet multifaceted types of human communication. A characteristic of all cultures, gossip is designed to ruin

DOI: 10.4324/9781003472162-2

an individual's or a group's reputation. It is a way to betray secrets. It is indeed "distilled malice."[2] Pope Francis comments:

> Gossip is so rotten. At the beginning, it seems to be something enjoyable and fun, like a piece of candy. But at the end, it fills the heart with bitterness and also poisons us. . . . I am convinced that if each one of us would purposely avoid gossip, at the end, we would become a saint![3]

Gossip gratifies the envy gossips feel towards others by denigrating their achievements; it provides gossips with a sense of power over people and a temporary feeling of bonding with their listeners. Individuals, by chattering about other people in a derogatory way, can avoid confronting serious issues within themselves and in the group itself. Gossip without a consciously evil intent is synonymous with what is commonly referred to as just "tittle-tattle." Without any prearranged planning, people tell stories or comment about the lives of people outside the group, but the effects on people's lives can be as disastrous as when gossip is intended to be injurious.

Defining Gossip

Because gossip is such a complex form of communication in cultures, it will be defined and explained in a series of propositions.[4]

Proposition 1: Gossip is "the negatively evaluative and morally laden verbal exchange concerning the conduct of absent third parties, that takes place within a bounded group of persons in a private setting."[5]

Gossip is the malicious and intimate interchange of prejudicial information within social groups such as by way of innuendo, whispering campaigns, allusion, insinuation, and hint.[6] For example, gossip is central to Shakespeare's play *Othello*. Iago intentionally spreads a lie that Othello's wife Desdemona is having an affair; Othello then murders his wife only to learn moments later that the gossip is false.

The malicious quality of gossip is startingly evident at times in the Old Testament. Joseph's brothers who are envious of their father's favouritism towards him gossip among themselves; they sell him to some slave traders, who take him to Egypt (Gen 37). Jeremiah stands out as a lonely, tragic person. He suffers the painful effects of the persistent gossip of his persecutors that leads to violence. He gives vent to his anguish, describing the abuse he suffers because of his role as a prophet, condemning his enemies and calling for his own vindication: "For I hear many whispering: 'Terror is all around! Denounce him! Let us denounce him!' All my close friends are watching for me to stumble" (Jer 20:10). Nothing timid here. He has been flung into prison, beaten, shackled, and even lowered down a well: "Why is my pain unceasing, my wound incurable, refusing to be healed?" (Jer 15:18). He even blames God for what is happening to him: "Truly, you are to me like a deceitful brook, like waters that fail" (Jer 15:18).

In Psalm 41 we read that the psalmist is in deep trouble. He has become ill and alienated from his friends because he has been slandered by their gossip: "All who hate me whisper together about me; they imagine the worst for me" (v.7). He is almost overwhelmed, demeaned, and alienated by their destructive whispering campaign: "They think a deadly thing has fastened on me, that I will not rise again from where I lie" (v.8). A fatal sickness grips him. His enemies maliciously believe that he is so afflicted that he deserves to die. Even his "bosom friend in whom I trusted, who ate of the bread, has lifted the heel against me" (v.9). Such is the cruel pain that gossip can cause. The psalm signally describes the vicious qualities that can characterize gossip.[7] In Psalm 64 the psalmist's antagonists are again persistently and spitefully gossiping about his virtuous behaviour. Borrowing language from the world of hunting, he graphically laments the controlling gossip of his enemies: They "whet their tongues like swords, shooting from ambush at the blameless; they shoot suddenly and without fear. They hold fast to their evil purpose; they talk of laying snares secretly" (vv.3-5).[8]

Proposition 2: Not only individuals gossip, cultures can be said to gossip also.

> Culture operates as a form of normative control beyond the volition of the individual. . . . While cultures might control people, it is almost unthinkable that people could control culture.
> (S. Barley, G. Meyer, D. Gash)[9]

Anthropologists speak of the "culture unconscious";[10] that is, culture is a "silent language";[11] we are rarely conscious of its powerful emotional and cognitive content and the way it shapes us how to feel, think, and behave. Culture has a life of its own. We live and die but the culture remains. It is so soundless that we do not know we are encased in culture until suddenly we become aware that it no longer exists! Therefore, people are inescapably shaped by the culture in which they live, by its many negative stereotypes of other people and cultures. Its power enters into every fibre of our being, without us ever being fully conscious of its influence.[12] "Men [sic] possess thoughts, but symbols possess men."[13] In our daily lives we do so many things without conscious deliberation; for example, we drive on the correct side of the road, and we sit automatically, as it were, in our favourite chair. Anthropologist Edward Hall adds this caution: "The cultural unconscious, like Freud's unconscious, not only controls man's [*sic*] actions but can be understood only by painstaking processes of detailed analysis."[14]

Thus our culture unconscious may influence who and what we gossip about. For example, institutional racism is the systematic allocation of power, resources, and work opportunities that benefit white people and disadvantage minority ethnic people.[15] It is the pattern of subjugation of Blacks by whites at the social level, resulting from the interaction of several social institutions such as systems of policing, the labour market, and education. One major reason why institutional racism continues is the fact that the culture has normalized it. People are unconsciously biased towards its maintenance. People who dare to challenge it become objects of gossip. Consider the incident where Jesus pauses by Jacob's Well in Samaria: "A Samaritan woman came to draw water, and Jesus said to her: 'Give me a drink'" (John 4:7). The Samarian woman replies sarcastically and uncritically mouthing the negative cultural prejudice against Jews: "'How is it that you, a Jew, ask a drink of me, a woman of Samaria?' (Jews do not share things in common with Samaritans.)" (John 4:9).

Proposition 3: Gossip and rumour differ.

"Rumour" and "gossip" *analytically* differ. A rumour is the unproven information about a significant event that is widely transmitted; it does not require the well-defined social network that gossip needs for its diffusion.[16] Rumours, unlike gossip, can be shared from person to person well distant from the original story.[17] Klaus Merton points out that in contrast to rumour, gossip takes place only among associates; it relates to a particular person who is known to all in a group; and the person gossiped about is absent.[18] Thus Donald Trump, when beginning his campaign to become president, openly and widely spread conspiracy rumours among familiar journalists and through tweets from 2011 that President Barack Obama was born in Asia, not America.[19]

Proposition 4: Jealousy and envy can motivate gossips.

O, beware, my Lord, of jealousy!
It is the green-ey'd monster, which doth mock
The meat it feeds on.
    (Shakespeare, *Othello*, act III, scene iii)

Envy and jealousy are almost taboo subjects in conversation and literature, even though they have bedevilled humankind from the beginning. Even social scientists have been hesitant to write about them, possibly because they are such unpalatable topics for writers and readers.[20] Yet envy and jealousy are common causes of the misuse of power in gossip and scapegoating. It is important to recognize the similarities and differences in these two words: "envy" and "jealousy."

Envy is the sadness a person or group feels because of what someone else has and the desire or wish that the other did not possess it. Envy operates when another person or group has better gifts, successes, or things than oneself, making one feel inferior or afraid of the consequences. There is a potentially destructive quality to envy. For example, if I cannot achieve the other's success, I will destroy that person's reputation through violence such as gossip or bullying. Anthropologist George Foster writes: "Envy is . . . a pan-human phenomenon . . . a particularly dangerous emotion, since it implies hostility, which leads to aggression and violence capable of destroying societies."[21] Envious persons fear people will notice their inferiority; he or she thinks that by destroying the object that causes envy, the problem will disappear. Envy, as a primitive, destructive disease, forms the foundation of many great works in English literature. In Robert Browning's poem "Soliloquy of the Spanish Cloister," a monk describes to himself ways in which his entire energy focuses on the destruction of the good Brother Lawrence. He dreams up ways to force the envied into heresy on his deathbed, while in the meantime furtively tearing off the buds of his melon plants. The speaker simply cannot stand Lawrence's simple goodness. Because he cannot achieve himself, he plans to destroy Lawrence.[22]

The psychoanalyst Melanie Klein in her study of envy diagnoses the infant's envy of the "creativity" of the good, life-giving, nourishing breast. The infant, who is dependent on it, resents that dependence and fantasizes about ingesting or destroying it.[23] It is this note of destructiveness that distinguishes envy from coveting and begrudging. To covet is to desire someone else's goods or qualities without, however, envying the owner. To begrudge is to want someone not to have the prestige or possessions that that person deserves. Unlike envy, coveting and begrudging do not connote the desire to see the envied person hurt, disgraced, or humbled.[24]

Jealousy, on the other hand, is also a potentially destructive sadness. It arises when a person fears losing or has already lost a meaningful status or relationship with another to a rival.[25] Jealousy assumes that what I fear losing, for example, property, prestige, I have by right; it is not caused by a feeling of inferiority, as is envy. Jealousy in gossip is often hidden under comments of moral indignation such as "Who are these people with the impudence to take away what rightly belongs to me!" The object of jealousy is what the person dreads they might lose, but with envy the spotlight is on the victim; that is, the person is envious of the person lucky enough to possess something held desirable. Foster writes that envy and jealousy thrive because it is thought that someone's gain in terms of prestige and position is possible only because of another's loss.[26] Both envy and jealousy are paralysing emotions that obstruct people from making rational judgements about reality. Fed by selfish or narcissistic desires,[27] the envious and the jealous person can become so consumed by anger or rage that nothing else matters but their own world of concern. A climate of suspicion and distrust is created in which deep friendships, collaboration, and teamwork become impossible.

Consider the example of the biblical prodigal son's brother. The prodigal son left home a self-centred adolescent but returned a mature adult, openly admitting his own weakness and begging forgiveness for his cruel rejection of his forgiving father. So the jealous and envious elder brother tries to gossip about his younger brother with his father, hoping, through the aid of gossip, to retrieve power over his father and his brother. The elder brother is jealous because he fears he is losing property for a celebratory feast to mark his brother's return; he is envious of the revitalized relationship between his father and wayward brother so he will do his best to destroy his brother's reputation with his father. Thus he gossips about his brother:

> Listen! For all these years I have been working like a slave for you, and I have never disobeyed your command; yet you have never given me even a young goat so I might celebrate with my friends. But when this son of yours came back, who has devoured your property . . . you killed the fatted calf for him.
>
> (Luke 15:29-30)

The father refuses to be party to the gossip.

Gossip and Violence

Proposition 5: Gossip is a form of violence.

The term "violence" does not have a standard or set definition. Violence, however, in this book means any action or lack of action of persons or cultures (including customs, institutions, structures) that are insensitive to and oppressive of human persons who have been created according to the divine image and likeness. Violence is not about damaging or destroying things. It is about abusing people.

Gossip is the most familiar and elementary form of masked violence. It is a disguised form of violence inasmuch as it is commonly prefaced with a comment like "You know, I do not wish him/her any harm, but . . ." (after which gossips proceed to do precisely what they say they will not do). Men and women are all equally capable of gossiping, but women over the centuries have more commonly been accused of this form of aggression. There is historically, however, an element of truth in this stereotype. Louise Collins comments: "the association of gossip with the feminine and a negative evaluation has a long history; in the English language, the term 'gossip' historically referred to a woman's circle of feminine friends."[28] Why is this so? Patricia Spacks notes that gossip can provide "a resource for the subordinated (anyone can *talk;* with a trusted listener, anyone can say anything), a crucial means of self-expression, a crucial form of solidarity" for the oppressed.[29] She writes: "Malicious gossip becomes an increasingly vital resource as other avenues of aggression are closed; and gossip as a means of solidarity also has special importance for the subordinated."[30] Women have been socially, politically, and economically oppressed for centuries in patriarchal societies, and one form of achieving and maintaining self-worth has been through gossip, particularly about the behaviour of men.

Proposition 6: Gossip is a type of bullying.

Bullying is an act of violence involving the abuse of power by individuals, groups, institutions, or cultures, so that individuals or groups not in a position to defend themselves are downgraded as human persons through being persistently subjected to threats of psychological, physical, or cultural violence, which weakens their self-confidence and self-esteem, thus facilitating their subjugation.[31] Bullies will use all kinds of intimidation including gossip to achieve their purpose. They aim to coerce people to do what they want them to do.

The impact of bullying on victims can be devastating. The words of the psalmist resonate with all victims down through the centuries, as he describes his suffering as a consequence of bullying: "Insults have broken my heart, so that I am in despair" (Ps 69:20); "I am utterly spent and crushed; I groan because of the tumult of my heart" (Ps 38:8); "I have become like a broken vessel" (Ps 31:12). The consequence of this abuse is that the victim's self-esteem and confidence are apt to disintegrate. I agree with Peter Randall that many adult bullies have Machiavellian talents in finding "devious ways of bringing pain to their victims without discredit to themselves."[32] And gossip is one such devious method.

Case Study

Vladimir Putin has co-opted the media to form a gossip clique to spread propaganda that Ukraine is a fake country, one that has no legitimacy; its leaders are neo-Nazis. Having dehumanized its citizens through such disinformation, he claims Russia can do anything to subjugate the Ukraine people.[33]

Gossip and Power

Proposition 6: Gossip is the misuse of power.

Gossip is a discourse about power and it can insidiously destroy trust in communities.[34] It gratifies the envy gossips feel towards others by denigrating the latter's achievements; it provides gossips with a feeling of control over others and a temporary bonding with their listeners. Individuals, by chattering about other people in a derogatory way, are able to avoid having to face serious issues within themselves and in the group itself. It flourishes in toxic cultures. "Gossip," writes philosopher Roland Barthes, "reduces the other to *he/she*. . . . The third-person pronoun is a wicked pronoun: it is the pronoun of non-person, it absents, it annuls."[35] Or, as Martin Buber writes, the interaction between the gossip and the victim is reduced to an I-It relationship, in which the victim is perceived merely as an object.[36]

Gossip outlines the boundaries of a group. It defines "us" and marginalizes "them," that is, those who are gossiped about. In all gossip at least three people (or groups) are involved: the gossip, the person(s) gossiped to, and the person or group gossiped about. The gossiper, motivated by envy or rage over other people's successes or failures, achieves at the moment of gossiping a sense of power over the person gossiped about. The person receiving the information not only shares this power but also feels flattered that he or she is trusted to hear the news. Friendship or alliance between the two parties is therefore reinforced. In brief, a yearning for power, or the desire to control others for one's own benefit, is at the heart of gossip. In the act of gossiping, the gossiper and the receiver of the information at least temporarily feel that they have the satisfaction of depowering the person or group gossiped about.

Gossip is a particularly safe form of power manipulation or aggression for its perpetrators, for two reasons: the gossip claims to be merely passing on information and so refuses to take responsibility for it, and it is all done in an atmosphere of trustful secrecy. The damage is done without anyone being called to testify to the information's objective accuracy. Sociologist Samuel Heilman speaks of gossip as "surreptitious aggression which enables one to wrest power, manipulate, and strike out at another without the other's being able to strike back."[37]

J. Edgar Hoover[38] deliberately gossiped with Robert Kennedy, Attorney General, by falsely branding Martin Luther King as a communist. Hoover also gossiped with Church leaders by spreading malicious rumours about King's personal life in an effort to stop civil rights' activism.[39] Hoover's harassment of King is a textbook example of gossip: "the use of false information in the irrational pursuit of a fictitious enemy."[40] Trygve Lie, the outgoing secretary-general of the United Nations, in order to retain his position deliberately spread false rumours among colleagues in 1953 about the sexual orientation of his nominated successor, Dag Hammarskjold.[41] Likewise with politicians, gossip can be used as a political weapon against opponents.

Case Study

While researching a small culture of an oppressed island people living on the fringe of a dominant Western society, I discovered the enormous power of gossip as a source of identity and also of social control. The islanders' sense of personal and cultural self-worth had been destroyed because of the paternalistic actions of a foreign colonial power over a period of a century. Representatives of this colonial government residing on the island, and the islanders themselves, constantly reinforced their separate identities and opposition to each other through gossip. Islanders, in the safe privacy of their dwellings or social gatherings, would recount true or false human failings of government officials. While recounting these lapses, the gossips would often laugh uproariously over the perceived stupidities of the officials and the government they represented. Gossip provided its agents with a renewed sense of self-worth and equality because the outsiders, despite their symbols of power, were nonetheless presented as stupid people, "not like us islanders." Islanders, however, were not aware that government officials and their families gossiped about them; the more outlandish the stories, the more convinced the outsiders were of their own sense of superiority and cohesion.

Proposition 7: Gossip causes a fragile bonding between the gossip and the person or group gossiped to; gossip destroys trust in relations.

Gossip has sometimes been defined as a cultural device used by individual(s) to further their own interests. The above case study stresses the relevance of this definition: the oppressed group is helped to make life bearable through its gossiping about the paternalistic colonial officials. Likewise, the more the government officers and their families gossiped about the islanders, the more confident they felt about their own sense of superiority. At the heart of gossip, therefore, there is an underlying streak of narcissism or self-interest ("My well-being must be enhanced, even if it means passing on lies or breaking secrets in order to ruin the reputation of others"). The receiver of the gossip, by assenting to listen, is expressing the same need for narcissistic satisfaction as the gossip.

The satisfaction and intimate alliances that come from being trusted to pass on gossip and to receive it are, however, very fragile. Because gossip is fundamentally a response to a narcissistic need for power over others, gossips know deep down that they in turn can readily become the objects of gossip. In the above example, the islanders were united in their dislike of government officials imposed on them by the dominant power, and the latter recognized this. However, the islanders themselves distrusted one another, often with considerable intensity. Because they had limited access to power and resources, they were always suspicious that fellow islanders were out to manipulate them to their disadvantage. So, through gossip, the islanders sought to express their envy of and desire to dominate one another, especially the more successful ones. The more scandalous the information, the more people sought to build up alliances or cliques of dependency through gossip. The more rapidly these alliances broke down, the greater the anger and sense of frustration among gossipers, and the greater the urge to develop more secure gossip alliances. Of course, when the object of the gossip learns what has happened, they are strongly tempted to make the gossiper the target of malicious talk.

Gossip destroys trust. Trust is a relationship between one or more persons, which has elements of openness and honesty, and a willingness to accept other(s) based on the opinion that the other party is both capable and dependable.[42] An organizational culture is said to be trusting when there is a kind of collective judgement that the people involved will act with honesty in negotiations and make "a good faith effort to behave in accordance with [their] commitments."[43] Where trust exists, people feel valued, and levels of job satisfaction are increased. Trust disintegrates when people fail to be transparently consistent in their behaviour. Gossips do not act transparently.

Proposition 8: Gossipers aim socially to control people according to their plans.

Since gossip can be a conversation about social rules that are being or have been violated, it can be a potent force in maintaining the status quo or conformity to a group's norms. Few people can withstand the consistent mockery of gossips. In the above example of the island people, a particularly disliked colonial bureaucrat became the target of increasingly malicious gossip, for he had gone beyond the bounds of tolerable behaviour for an outsider. After a while he could no longer take the silences, stares, or ridiculing comments of the islanders, so he was forced to leave the island. Of course, the government official could blame no particular person for the gossip, so court action for defamation was impossible. This case study of the removal of a particularly objectionable colonial official illustrates that gossip can sometimes have a positive function. However, more commonly gossip or the fear of it is not only destructive to an individual's reputation but is also apt to inhibit or block any justified effort to change the status quo within a culture.

In many cultures people often hesitate to introduce much-needed agricultural or health changes because they fear that gossip will socially isolate them and their families. I have seen people with innovative gifts tolerate near-starvation conditions in parts of the South Pacific with great agricultural potential, simply because they felt they could not withstand the consequences of the gossip that would have spread if they had dared to introduce better methods of cultivation. Particularly within traditional cultures, gossips are thought to have the assistance, if they wish, of witchcraft powers as will be explained later. It is believed that gossips can invoke secret magical forces to destroy or harm people daring to question the cultural status quo. Would-be innovators, believing in the world of magical powers, require enormous courage to withstand the wrath of "supernatural" forces generated against them through gossip. My own experience of situations of this kind is that few can withstand the pressures to conform to the old ways of doing things.

Gossips Shame

Proposition 9: Gossips shame their victims.[44]

"Shaming" refers to all social actions, including gossip, that express "disapproval [and] have the intention or effect of invoking remorse in the person being shamed and/or condemnation by others who become aware of the shaming."[45] For example, the victim may discover that they are being shamed through gossip by the ways they are shunned or in other ways mistreated by the gossiper's confidants. True, shaming can be good, for example, when people feel coerced to act justly, but it can also be bad when people are unjustly affected. In this book shaming is being used in this second sense, namely as a powerful form of gossip.

Being the object of constant shaming techniques may forever undermine a person's social standing, or even group membership, sometimes forcing the victim to self-harm.[46] Sociologist Chie Nakane, writing on the way Japanese individuals are controlled by the fear of gossipy shaming, notes:

> The feeling that "I must do this because A and B also do it" or "they will laugh at me unless I do such-and-such" rules the life of the individual with greater force than any other consideration and thus has a deep effect on decision-making.[47]

This has an immense potential for an insidious form of violence against people. As Nakane says, "the power at the top, always a dominant group and never an individual, succeeds in imposing its aims, with even the law powerless to offer any check."[48] An example of this is the traditional custom of *murahachibu* (social ostracism), which is a form of "silent" gossip.

When surplus labour is to be shed, a company's personnel department may encourage workers to ostracize those targeted for dismissal. A middle manager, for example, who has worked for the company for years fails to receive his cup of green tea from the office lady. A week later he is removed. It finally dawns on the victim that he or she is being collectively mocked by their work colleagues, and when it becomes unbearable, they leave. This form of quiet gossip is common in the Japanese corporate world.[49]

"To feel shame" means that the mocking or gossip has hit home. It is that piercing feeling of humiliation that public exposure causes, something far worse than feeling embarrassed, which is a short-lived experience of discomfort because some social norm has been ignored. Shame occurs when a person or a group feels they are negatively evaluated by others (and even by themselves as measured by their personal standards), and manifests itself through behaviour such as speech disruption, lowered or averted gaze, blushing, or barely audible speech, the desire to hide.[50]

Anthropologist Maori Marsden describes the meaning of "being shamed" for Maori people. *Whakamaa* (shamed) is the experience of being looked down upon by others. People show they are *whakamaa* in external behaviour that ranges from limited responsiveness and monosyllabic answers, through withdrawal into the self while physically present, to actual running away from threatening situations. They are exterior expressions of inward disintegration or overall loss of self-worth because "you know you are not what you should be within your group. . . . You have a certain place in society, and anything that takes you off your base in cultural terms causes *whakamaa*."[51] St Thomas Aquinas, following Aristotle, argued that the desire to act violently is the result of having been shamed; people feel justified in getting revenge for having been treated with contempt and disrespect.[52]

Shame is about our status as a person or *who we are*; it is about identity. A violator such as a gossip aims to destroy the victim's sense of social/personal self-worth. Once, when I was researching the socioeconomic effects of credit unions in rural Fiji, I asked a group of Fijians what it was like to be in the presence of British colonial officials. One informant replied:

> When I approach a white official I suddenly feel inferior all over. I have done nothing wrong, but he tells me by the way he looks that I am worth nothing in society. You know he and others are laughing at we Fijians behind our backs. My knees shake and my heart beats hard.

The haughty behaviour of the official reflected the colonial gossipy racist culture of his day. Stephen Pattison describes the horrible impact of society's shaming:

> The society that shames groups or individuals does not value or want them. Indeed, shamed, defiled or stigmatised individuals and groups

may be positively feared and actively rejected. Perhaps more damagingly, they are unacknowledged . . . [Any] person or group that is habitually shamed will be dehumanised.[53]

Shame emerges from the public uncovering of vulnerability, but guilt is something private that follows a sense of failing to maintain private and internal standards.[54] The complementary value of shame is *honour*. The gossip wants to maintain their honour while denigrating their victims. In fact, the honour-shame dynamic acts as a lingua franca across the world, but every culture has its unique expression.[55] Honour is a person's or group's sense of self-worth and the public, social acceptance of that assessment. Honour is the foundation of one's reputation, of one's social status in community: "Honour is the value of a person in his own eyes, but also in the eyes of his society."[56] There are various ways people claim or maintain honour in order to avoid feeling shamed. Deceit is one way people seek to maintain honour.

Richard Nixon, in an effort to hide the Watergate break-in scandal, instructed his staff to cover up what had happened to protect the honour of the presidency. For him the end justified the means. Even when he sacrificed some of his closest aides, he still claimed that this was necessary in order to maintain the status of presidency. President Trump turned lying into an art form to uphold his honour through creating rumours, gossip, and supporting conspiracy theories. Self-praise is also a way to reaffirm one's honour in most societies. For example, in Western societies, the ritual begins with "[t]his may sound like boasting, but. . . ." The Pharisee at prayer in the Temple asserts his honourable status before God by self-praise: "I am not grasping, unjust, adulterous like everyone else, and particularly I am not like this tax collector here" (Luke 18:11). Jesus, of course, uses the incident to declare that the criteria of the truly honourable person are not those set by the Pharisees (Luke 18:14).

Gossip and Cultural Upheaval

Proposition 10: Gossip intensifies in times of stressful cultural upheaval or chaos.

Disruptive experiences of chaos become catalysts for anxiety-creating radical cultural changes. Anthropologists are turning to the chaos theory of physics and applying its basic assumptions to the study of cultures. Broadly defined the theory is "the science of process rather than state, of becoming rather than being . . . [resulting in] a science of the global nature of systems."[57] It means that chaos and order interact and are always on the borders of the other. The movement of change is not smooth, but lurching, and its necessary impetus is stress. At certain points, changes may amplify into disturbances so profound and deep that a culture breaks apart, but may eventually reconfigure itself into a much more complex system.[58]

Within each human person, there is an unlimited yearning for liberty, but this desire competes with a longing for *normality, order*, and the *familiar*. Ultimately it is the latter that most often wins. We may even put up with persecution *provided* it is predictable! As Peter Berger writes, culture protects people from the awesome insecurities and meaninglessness of chaos (*anomy*). Culture (*nomos*) is

> an area of meaning carved out of a vast mass of meaninglessness, a small clearing of lucidity in a formless, dark, almost ominous jungle. ... Every *nomos* is an edifice erected in the face of the potent and alien forces of chaos. This chaos must be kept at bay at all costs.[59]

Anxiety intensifies. Chaos is feared. Order must return and prevail. Anthropologist Clifford Geertz agrees:

> Man (*sic*) depends upon symbols and symbol systems with a dependence so great as to be decisive for his creatural viability and, as a result, his sensitivity to even the remotest indication that they may prove unable to cope with one or another aspect of experience raises within him the gravest sort of anxiety.[60]

It is not surprising, therefore, that anyone who questions the cultural status quo or creates chaos, for example, an innovator, a whistleblower, can become the object of violence such as gossip, scapegoating, or marginalization; "the individual who strays seriously from the socially defined programs can be considered not only a fool or a knave but a madman."[61] The relationship between cultural chaos, gossip, and conspiracy theorizing is further explained in subsequent chapters.

Proposition 11: The internet provides boundless opportunities for uncontrolled gossip; we are in the Age of Disinformation.

For all its ephemerality, the internet is a reservoir of deathless resentment and grudges, in which loners and fanatics find solace or a mirror for their yearnings. Calumnies and conspiracies of all kinds now live on for ever.[62]

In the contemporary world in which cultures are in constant and disruptive change, and technical surveillance systems become widely available,[63] gossip as a business operation has reached massive proportions. Scandal or gossip magazines, purporting to "tell all" about the rich, powerful, and famous, lock in on people's deep-seated need to experience power over others. In the secrecy of their rooms, readers can feel at once envious of and superior to the rich and powerful ("they may be rich and powerful, but I know all about them"). The reader experiences a passing satisfaction of having inside knowledge of, and thus power over, others.[64]

Dangerous fake news is not a new reality. Benjamin Franklin protested that "tearing your private character to flitters" could be achieved by anyone with a printing press. Freedom of the press, he complained, had come to mean "the liberty of affronting, calumniating, and defaming one another."[65] Faking information was normal in the final quarter of the nineteenth century, but as "the century turned, however, journalistic practices began to coalesce into informal codes of conduct."[66] With the arrival of internet technology, the informal codes ceased to function. Ed Cooper describes the consequences:

> People retreated into likeminded bubbles of groupthink, autocrats entrenched their rule through social media and knowledge was supplanted by "alternative facts" that marched back and forth across the internet while truth was still putting its pants on. . . . Disinformation is a virus that spreads contagious information from person to person, leaving a trail of human wreckage in its wake.[67]

People could now gossip without restraint, including conspiracy theories anonymously and globally. It does not matter whether the information is true or false. Rather, the key issue is, will the internet posting provoke a powerful reaction or outrage or not?[68] The social media giants, such as Facebook, Twitter, and Google, for the most part refuse to curb the disinformation. For example, so many Covid-related lies and conspiracies appeared on their platforms that Vivek Murphy, the US surgeon general, published a formal advisory in July 2022 that the platforms "enabled misinformation to poison our information environment, with little accountability to their users." He termed this an "urgent crisis."[69]

Scriptural Critique

St Benedict, the great sixth-century religious founder, left his monks in no uncertainty about the dangers of gossip when he wrote his Rule: "If you desire true and eternal life, keep your tongue free from vicious talk and your lips from all deceit; turn away from evil and do good."[70] But the monks could not heed this warning and every other aspect of his Rule if they failed to contemplate the Scriptures as he wrote in the Prologue: "Listen carefully to the master's instructions and attend to them with the ear of your heart."

So also for us in these contemporary times. I have clarified the anthropology of gossip as the breeding ground of conspiracy theorizing. Now is the time with this material as background to contemplate what the scriptures say about gossip, and they say a great deal because examples of gossip abound and are critiqued in the Scriptures. Only then will we be ready to tackle the public expression of gossip, namely conspiracy theories and their malevolent qualities.

Old Testament

In the Old Testament the serpent in the garden gossips with Eve about God with evil intent and dire consequences: "But the serpent said to the woman, 'You will not die; for God knows that when you eat of it your eyes will be opened, and you will be like God, knowing good and evil'" (Gen 3:4-5). Eve believes the gossip and convinces Adam to do the same. The resultant violation of God's commandment not to eat the fruit immediately leads to their punishment. The brothers of Joseph gossip about him, even planning to kill him (Gen 37:18-20). The Book of Leviticus condemns gossip: "You shall not go around as a slanderer among your people, and you shall not profit by the blood of your neighbour: I am the Lord" (Lev 19:16).

Elsewhere synonyms for gossip such as "slander," "mocking" abound and are condemned: "The wise heart will heed commandments, but the babbling fool will come to ruin" (Prov 10: 8); "One who secretly slanders a neighbour I will destroy" (Ps 101:5); "You give free rein for evil, and your tongue frames deceit. You sit and speak against your kin; you slander your own mother's child" (Ps 50:19-20); "But at my stumbling they gather in glee, they gathered together against me; ruffians whom I did not know tore at me without ceasing; they impiously mocked more and more, gnashing at me with their teeth" (Ps 35:15-16).

In Psalm 88 the petitioner feels desperately shamed by his friends who shun him because of his illness. His friends in their gossip assert his illness is due to some sinful action on his part and therefore sun him. It has "caused my companions to shun me"; it has "made me a thing of horror to them" and now he is "darkness" (Ps 88: 8, 18). The Israelites in their journeying to the promised land give free rein to gossiping about God and God reacts:

> But you were unwilling to go up [to Canaan]. You rebelled against the command of the Lord your God; you grumbled in your tents and said, "It is because the Lord hates us that he has brought us out of the land of Egypt, to hand us over to the Amorites to destroy us. . . . When the Lord heard your words, he was wrathful and swore: Not one of

these – not one of this evil generation – shall see the good land that I swore to your ancestors.

(Deut 1:26-27)

New Testament

In the New Testament there are significant references to the dangers of gossip.[71] The lesson? Believers must not be gossipers! Herod, for his own cruel ends, seeks to engage the wise men in gossip, but they break its spell by being warned in a dream not to cooperate further (Matt 2:7-12). In the account of the temptation of Jesus in the desert, the devil calculatingly seeks to involve Jesus in gossip about God. Jesus will have none of it: "Away with you, Satan! for it is written, 'Worship the Lord your God, and serve only him'" (Matt 4:10).

Jesus later condemns his critics for gossiping maliciously behind his back. He publicly names the prejudices in their gossip: "For John came neither eating nor drinking, and they say, 'He has a demon'; the Son of Man came eating and drinking, and they say, 'Look, a glutton and a drunkard, a friend of tax collectors and sinners!'" (Matt 11:18-18). On another occasion, Jesus identifies the whispering campaign against him and upbraids those responsible for it: "Do not complain among yourselves" (John 6:43). They scorned his teaching: "Is not this Jesus, the son of Joseph, whose father and mother we know?" (John 6:42).

St Paul condemned gossips as evil: "Full of envy, murder, strife, deceit, craftiness they are gossips . . . inventors of evil" (Rom 1:29); and "gossips" say "what they should not say" (1 Tim 5:13); "Avoid the profane chatter and contradictions of what is falsely called knowledge" (1 Tim 6:20); "Avoid profane chatter, for it will lead people into more and more impiety" (2 Tim: 2:16). He condemned the gossip he feared still existed among the Corinthians: "I fear that there may perhaps be quarrelling, jealousy, anger, selfishness, slander, gossip, conceit, and disorder" (2 Cor 12:20).

St James writes to a church community that is confronted with discrimination and economic oppression. As one of his main concerns is the need for unity among believers, he attacks in trenchant language those who gossip among themselves:

> How great a forest is set ablaze by a small fire! And the tongue is a fire. The tongue is placed among our members as a world of iniquity; it stains the whole body, sets on fire the cycle of nature, and is itself set on fire by hell.
>
> (James 3:5-6)[72]

James is pessimistic about human efforts to control speech: "no one can tame the tongue – a restless evil, full of deadly poison. With it we bless the Lord and Father, and with it we curse those who are made in the likeness of God" (James 3:8).

Honour, Shame, and Gossip

By understanding the dynamic interaction between honour and shame in the scriptures, we are able to better appreciate their role in gossip (see *Proposition 10*).[73] Honour is a person's or group's sense of self-worth and the public, social acceptance of that assessment. There are various ways people claim or maintain honour in their community, and each may involve violence or abuse of power. Shaming refers to social actions, such as gossiping, which aim to make the victim feel demeaned, worthless, or socially a non-person.

In the Old Testament, Israel's claim to honour is its intimate relationship to God (Ps 8:5). As long as God maintains protective care, Israel experiences honour, but when the people are crushed by enemies, it is a sign to them that the special relationship has ceased and they experience deep shame (Jer 46:25). In the New Testament, Christ is out to show that his definition of honour is culturally radically different from that of his listeners; Jesus aims to establish a new mythological foundation for all human cultures. A person with authority at the time of Christ was expected for the sake of honour to dominate and demean others such as servants or citizens. Jesus verbally and in action asserted that his followers must adopt a different approach to honour (Mark 10:42-43).

Jesus had to submit to a series of show trials before the Sanhedrin council (a court made up of the local elite frightened that their prestige with the people was threatened [Luke 22:66-71]), before Pilate (Luke 23:13-25), and before Herod (Luke 23:8-12). All aimed to shame Jesus publicly in the eyes of the people, and successfully to re-establish the honour of the accusers. The shaming of Jesus so that he became a non-person continued with mocking, flogging, and the humiliating carrying of the cross.[74] According to Jewish culture, Jesus should have felt terribly shamed because he submitted to death and worse, death by crucifixion. Death by crucifixion was considered to be the cruellest and most shameful capital punishment. He was mocked as a king, onlookers ridiculed him, and his friends left him. Jesus was no longer a man of honour according to the local cultural code,[75] yet, in this action, Jesus establishes a new code of honour: sacrifice of oneself for others out of love.

The true Christian is one who is prepared to be reviled, even to die, that others may live. The Beatitudes turn the contemporary culture's code of honour upside down: "Blessed" means "how honorable" – thus,

"How honorable are you when people hate you . . . on account of the Son of Man" (Luke 6:22). Likewise, whoever loves their enemies is truly honorable; not to love them is shameful (Luke 6:27).

Summary Points

- Behind conspiracy theorizing in the public forum, there is always the supportive, energizing, and covert world of gossip. Not only does gossip help to shape conspiracy theories but it also ensures that they quickly spread increasingly aided by the internet. The malevolent power of these theories cannot be appreciated without an intimate awareness of how gossip operates.
- Gossip as an act of violence is designed to ruin an individual's or a group's reputation. It gratifies the envious and revengeful feelings gossips feel towards others by denigrating the victim's achievements; it provides gossips with a temporary sense of power over people and a feeling of bonding with their listeners.
- Gossip in its many forms, for example, whispering campaigns, flourishes especially in turbulent times.
- Shaming refers to social actions, such as gossiping, which aim to make the victim feel demeaned, worthless, or socially a non-person. Individuals and groups in order to maintain their honor or social status will use gossip to shame others.
- The scriptures contain many examples of gossip and its malevolent consequences. For example, Christ himself was frequently the object of gossip through whispering shaming campaigns.

Discussion Questions

1 St James writes of gossip:

> no one can tame the tongue – a restless evil, full of deadly poison. With it we bless the Lord and Father, and with it we curse those who are made in the likeness of God. . . . How great a forest is set ablaze by a small fire! And the tongue is a fire. The tongue is placed among our members as a world of iniquity; it stains the whole body, sets on fire the cycle of nature, and is itself set on fire by hell.
> (James 3:5-6, 8)

From your experience do you feel this is an adequate description of the consequences of gossip as described in this chapter?

2 Read the story of the Prodigal Son (Luke 15:11-31). In what ways do you think this is a story about different views of honor and shame?

Notes

1. All scripture quotations are from the New Revised Standard Version of the Bible.
2. Christopher M. Elias, *Gossip Men* (Chicago: Chicago University Press, 2021), 13.
3. Pope Francis, www.ncregister.com/daily-news/pope-francis-gossip-is-poisonous (Accessed June 2, 2015).
4. For helpful insights into the nature and complexity of gossip, see Katherine E. Sheffield, "'Longing in Vain to Climb into the Ducal Bed': Gossip and Rumor in Orderic Vitalis' Ecclesiastical History." Ph.D Dissertation, (University of Missouri-Columbia, 2016), 1–41. (PDF).
5. Niko Besnier, *Gossip: And the Everyday Production of Politics* (Honolulu: University of Hawaii Press, 2009), 13.
6. Anthropologists differ about the function and place of gossip in social groups. The structuralist-functionalist approach emphasizes the role of gossip in reinforcing cohesion in groups. Anthropologist Max Gluckman notes that in many non-literate cultures gossip does not necessarily have the pejorative meaning because it is often the only way to obtain information that defines and unites societies. See Max Gluckman, "Gossip and Scandal," *Current Anthropology*, no. 3 (1963): 307–16. The transactional view downplays the cohesion emphasis and stresses the role of gossip in providing opportunities for individuals to manipulate customs for their personal advantage. See Robert Paine, "What Is Gossip About? An Alternative Hypothesis," *Man: Journal of the Royal Anthropological Institute*, vol. 2, no. 2 (1967): 278–85. The symbolic-interactionists, however, emphasize that gossip is primarily a way to mislead others for personal or group advantage. Gossip can have dramatic consequences for victims, a point that the first two views do not address. See Niko Besnier, "Gossip," ed. David Levinson and Melvin Ember, *Encyclopedia of Cultural Anthropology*, Vol. 2 (New York: Henry Holt, 1996), 544–7; John Haviland, *Gossip, Reputation and Knowledge in Zinacantan* (Chicago: University of Chicago Press, 1977) and Peter J. Wilson, "Filcher of Good Names: An Enquiry Into Anthropology and Gossip," *Man*, vol. 9. no. 1 (1974): 93–102. Gossip is used throughout this book in this last most commonly accepted pejorative sense.
7. See Walter Brueggemann and William H. Bellinger, *Psalms* (Cambridge: Cambridge University Press, 2014), 199–202.
8. See Brueggemann and Bellinger, *Psalms*, 280–3.
9. S.R. Barley, G. W. Meyer, and D.C. Gash, "Cultures of Culture: Academics, Practitioners, and the Pragmatics of Normative Control," *Administrative Science Quarterly*, no. 33 (1988): 44.
10. See Terry Eagleton, *Culture* (New Haven, CT: Yale University Press, 2016), 49–95. See comments by Susan Greenwood and Erik D. Goodwyn, *Magical Consciousness: An Anthropological and Neurobiological Approach* (New York: Routledge, 2016), 64–78.

11 See Edward Hall, *The Silent Language* (New York: Doubleday, 1959).
12 See Gerald A. Arbuckle, *Earthing the Gospel: An Inculturation Handbook for Pastoral Workers* (Maryknoll, NY: Orbis Books, 1990), 26.
13 Max Lerner, *The Ideas of the Ice Age* (New York: Viking, 1941), 235. See comments by David I. Kertzer, *Ritual, Politics and Power* (New Haven: Yale University Press, 1988), 5–6.
14 Edward Hall, *Beyond Culture* (Garden City: Anchor Press/Doubleday, 1977), 43.
15 See Gerald A. Arbuckle, *The Pandemic and the People of God: Cultural Impacts and Pastoral Responses* (Maryknoll, NY: Orbis Books, 2021), 153–90.
16 See Ralph L. Rosnow and Alan J. Kimmel, "Rumor," ed. Alan E. Kazdin, *Encyclopedia of Psychology*, Vol. 7 (New York: Oxford University Press, 2000), 122–3; Prashant Bordia and Nicholas Difonzo, "Problem Solving in Social Interactions on the Internet: Rumor as Social Cognition," *Social Psychology Quarterly*, vol. 67, no. 1 (2004): 33–49.
17 See Hans-Joachim Neubauer, *The Rumor: A Cultural History*, trans. Christian Braun (London: Free Association Books, 1999), 3.
18 See Klaus Merten as cited by Axel Gelfert, "Rumor, Gossip, and Conspiracy Theories," ed. Greg Dalziel, *Rumor and Communication in Asia in the Internet Age* (Abingdon: Routledge, 2013), 27; see Pamela J. Stewart and Andrew Strathern, *Witchcraft, Sorcery, Rumors, and Gossip* (Cambridge: Cambridge University Press, 2004), 38–9.
19 See Michael Butter, *The Nature of Conspiracy Theories* (Cambridge: Polity, 2020), 144–7.
20 See Helmut Schoeck, *Envy: A Theory of Social Behaviour* (Indianapolis: Liberty Press, 1966), 12–16.
21 George M. Foster, "The Anatomy of Envy: A Study in Symbolic Behavior," *Current Anthropology*, vol. 13, no. 2 (1972): 165.
22 See Robert Browning, *Selected Poems by Robert Browning*, ed. W.T. Hutchins (London: Longmans, Green and Co, 1937), 133.
23 See Melanie Klein, *Envy and Gratitude and Other Works* (London: Virago, 1988), 176–235.
24 See Gary R. Collins, *Overcoming Anxiety* (Wheaton: Key Press, 1973), 108–9.
25 See Schoeck, *Envy*, 115–17.
26 See Foster, "Anatomy of Envy," 165–202.
27 See Neville Symington, *Emotion and Spirit* (London: Cassell, 1994), 115–27.
28 Louise Collins, "Gossip: A Feminine Defense," eds. Robert F. Goodman and Aaron Ben-Ze'ev, *Good Gossip* (Lawrence: University Press of Kansas, 1994), 114.
29 Patricia Meyer Sparks, *Gossip* (New York: Alfred A. Knopf, 1985), 5.
30 Sparks, *Gossip*, 13.
31 See Gerald A. Arbuckle, *Dealing With Bullies* (London: St Pauls Publishing, 2003), 17–25.

32 Peter Randall, *Bullying in Adulthood: Perpetrators and Victims* (London: Routledge, 1996), 7.
33 See Anne Applebaum, "'They're Not Human Beings': Ukraine and the Words That Lead to Mass Murder," *The Atlantic* (June, 2022), 11–15; Sergei Guriev and Daniel Treisman argue that Putin is a "spin dictator"; that is, he claims to be a democrat and eschew open repression and violence within Russia. At the same time he masterfully uses modern communications technology for propaganda, spin, and manipulation, all aimed at concealing or camouflaging his brutal repression. *Spin Dictators: The Changing Face of Tyranny in the 21st Century* (Princeton: Princeton University Press, 2022), 16–17.
34 See Spacks, *Gossip*, 68.
35 Roland Barthes, *A Lover's Discourse*, trans. Richard Howard (New York: Hill and Wang, 1978), 185.
36 See Martin Buber, *Between Man and Man* (New York: Routledge, 2002), xii.
37 Samuel C. Heilman, *Synagogue Life: A Study of Symbolic Interaction* (Chicago: University of Chicago Press, 1976), 156.
38 Christopher Elias describes how J. Edgar Hoover, Joseph McCarthy, and Roy M. Cohn used gossip for political aims. *Gossip Men*, 15–16. The aides of the former disgraced governor of New York Eliot Spitzer "circulated unfounded allegations that Richard Grasso, who was the head of the New York Stock Exchange and one of Mr Spitzer's many bugbears, was sleeping with his secretary." "Lexington: The Hypocrites' Club," *The Economist* (March 15, 2008), 54.
39 See Fred Powell, *Free At Last? The Civil Rights Movement and the People Who Made It* (Boston: Little Brown Press, 1991), 610.
40 Ted Morgan, *Reds: McCarthyism in Twentieth-Century America* (New York: Random House, 2003), 566.
41 See Roger Lipsey, *Hammarskjold: A Life* (Ann Arbor: University of Michigan Press, 2013), 95–108.
42 See Rocky J. Dwyer, "Benchmarking as a Process for Demonstrating Organizational Trustworthiness?" *Management Decision*, vol. 46, no. 8 (2008): 1210–229.
43 Dwyer, "Benchmarking," 1212.
44 See Gerald A. Arbuckle, *Violence, Society, and the Church: A Cultural Approach* (Collegeville, MN: Liturgical Press, 2004), 79–93.
45 John Braithwaite, *Crime, Shame and Reintegration* (Cambridge: Cambridge University Press, 1989), 100.
46 See Bronislaw Malinowski, *Crime and Custom in Savage Society* (London: Kegan Paul, 1926), 77–9.
47 Chie Nakane, *Japanese Society* (Harmondsworth: Pelican, 1973), 155–6.
48 Nakane, *Japanese Society*, 156.
49 See Takie Sugiyama Lebra, *Japanese Patterns of Behavior* (Honolulu: University of Hawaii Press, 1976), 110–36.
50 See Thomas J. Scheff, "Shame and Conformity: The Difference-Emotion System," *American Sociological Review*, vol. 53, no. 3 (1988): 395–405.

51 Maori Marsden quoted by Joan Metge, *In and Out of Touch: Whakamaa in Cross-Cultural Context* (Wellington: Victoria University Press, 1986), 77.
52 See Thomas Aquinas, *Summa Theologiae* I-II Q. 47. 1.
53 Stephen Pattison, *Shame: Theory, Therapy, Theology* (Cambridge: Cambridge University Press, 2000), 183. See also Donald L. Nathanson, *Shame and Pride* (New York: W.W. Norton, 1992), 217–35.
54 See Lenore Terr, *Too Scared to Cry: Psychic Trauma in Childhood* (Grand Rapids: Harper & Row, 1990), 113–14. Thomas Ryan offers a pastorally helpful insight about shame's potential for healing: "Shame's energy, if tapped and guided, contributes to the healing and integration of the person (in wholeness and holiness) and heightened emotional sensitivity (whether interpersonally or trans-personally)." "Transforming Shame: Strategies in Spirituality and Prayer," eds. Claude-Helene Mayer and Elizabeth Vanderheiden, *The Bright Side of Shame: Transforming and Growing Through Practical Applications in Cultural Contexts* (Cham, Switzerland: Springer, 2019), 187–98.
55 See Jayson Georges and Mark D. Baker, *Ministering in Honor-Shame Cultures* (Downers Grove, IL: IVP Academic, 2016), 2–48.
56 Julian Alfred Pitt-Rivers, "Honour and Shame," ed. John G. Peristiany, *Honour and Shame: The Values of Mediterranean Society* (Chicago: University of Chicago Press, 1966), 21.
57 James Glieck, *Chaos: Making a New Science* (New York: Penguin, 1987), 5.
58 See Mark S. Mosko and Frederick H. Damon, *On the Order of Chaos: Social Anthropology and the Science of Chaos* (New York: Berghahn, 2005).
59 Peter Berger, *The Sacred Canopy: Elements of a Sociological Theory of Religion* (New York: Doubleday, 1969), 23.
60 Clifford Geertz, *The Interpretation of Cultures* (Columbus: Free Press, 1963), 99.
61 Berger, *The Sacred Canopy*, 23.
62 "Never-Ending Story," *The Economist* (August 20, 2022), 14.
63 See Shoshana Zuboff, *The Age of Surveillance Capitalism* (London: Profile Books, 2019).
64 See Patricia Mellencamp, *High Anxiety: Catastrophe, Scandal, Age and Comedy* (Bloomington: Indiana University Press, 1992), 194–229.
65 Benjamin Franklin cited by Jonathan Rauch, *The Constitution of Knowledge* (Washington, DC: Brookings Institutional Press, 2021), 121.
66 Rauch, *The Constitution of Knowledge*, 122.
67 Ed Cooper, *Facts and Other Lies: Welcome to the Disinformation Age* (Sydney: Allen & Unwin, 2022), 3.
68 See Max Fisher, *The Chaos Machine: The Inside Story of How Social Media Rewired Our Minds and Our World* (Sydney: Quercus, 2022), 92.
69 Vivek Murphy cited by Fisher, *The Chaos Machine*, 331–2. An attempt in 2020 by the Australian government to regulate Facebook failed.
70 Timothy Fry, *The Rule of St Benedict in English* (Collegeville, MN: Liturgical Press, 1982), 18.

71 See John W. Daniels, Jr., "Gossip in the New Testament," *Biblical Theology Bulletin*, vol. 42, no. 4 (2012): 204–13, and "Gossip in John's Gospel and the Social Processing of Jesus' Identity," *Journal of Early Christian History*, vo. 1, no. 2 (2017): 9–29. www.doi.org/10.1080/2222582X.2011.11877242 (Accessed July 19, 2019).
72 See Peter H. Davids, "James, The Letter of," eds. Bruce M. Metzger and Michael D. Coogan, *The Oxford Companion to the Bible* (Oxford: Oxford University Press, 1993), 341.
73 See *Biblical Values and Their Meaning*, eds. John J. Pilch and Bruce J. Malina (Peabody: Hendrickson, 1993), 95–104; Saul M. Olyan, "Honor, Shame, and Covenant Relations in Ancient Israel," *Journal of Biblical Literature*, vol. 115, no. 2 (1996): 201–18; Thomas Ryan, *Shame, Hope and the Church: A Journey With Mary* (Strathfield: St Pauls Publications, 2020), 39–80.
74 See Bruce J. Malina and Richard L. Rohrbaugh, *Social Science Commentary on the Synoptic Gospels* (Minneapolis: Fortress Press, 1992), 406–8.
75 See John J. Pilch, "Death With Honor: The Mediterranean Style Death of Jesus in Mark," *Biblical Theology Bulletin*, vol. 25, no. 2 (1995): 65–70.

2 Conspiracy Theorizing Uncovered[1]

> Conspiracy theories resist traditional canons of proof because they reduce highly complex phenomena to simple causes.
> (Michael Barkun)[2]

> The penchant for conspiracy theories seems stronger today than it was during the Birchers' heyday in the 1960s.
> (James Mann)[3]

> Ending political violence . . . means rebuking the conspiracy theorist who uses the rhetoric of truth-seeking to obscure what's real.
> (Adrienne LaFrance)[4]

> Falsehood flies, and the truth comes limping after it; so that when men come to be undeceived, it is too late; the jest is over, and the tale has had its effect.
> (Jonathan Swift)[5]

This chapter explains that:

- How gossip is a breeder of conspiracy theories.
- Conspiracy theories thrive in chaos.
- They can cause enormous harm to people.
- Conspiracy beliefs defy rational questioning.
- Faith in Christ Redeemer is the ultimate so

When the private world of gossip moves into the public arena, we can have conspiracy theorizing with its malevolent qualities. Consider this example. The evangelist St Matthew recounts the incident following the death of Christ when the chief priests, after gossiping among themselves, demanded that Pilate place guards at the tomb. They were frightened that the disciples of Jesus would steal the body of Christ "and tell the people, 'He has been raised from the dead'" (Matt 27:64).

When an angel "came and rolled back the stone . . . For fear of him the guards shook and became like dead men" (Matt 28:4). Then "some of the guard went into the city and told the chief priests everything that had happened" (Matt 28:11). The chief priests with the elders once more gossiped among themselves devising a conspiracy theory telling the guard, "You must say, 'His disciples came by night and stole him away while we were asleep'" (Matt 28:13). The guards did what they had been told, having been bribed with "a large sum of money" (Matt 28:12). They left the evil plotters and publicly spread the conspiracy theory that the disciples had stolen the body of Christ: "And this story is still told among the Jews to this day" (Matt 28:15). From gossip to conspiracy theorizing!

The purpose of this chapter is now to describe the nature and power of conspiracy theorizing types, the harm they cause, and why they are so difficult pastorally to contradict. Subsequent chapters will go more deeply into particular issues raised here.

Today we are in a golden age of conspiracy theorizing. True, such theorizing has been around for centuries. However, with the rapid spread of internet technology there is now a tsunami of conspiracy theories of all kinds. Online platforms with little or no restraints are making conspiracies more poisonous, more forceful, more violently harmful (see *Proposition 12*, Chapter 1). Also the present surge of conspiracy theories is partly related to the rise of popular movements, in that there are often structural parallels between populist leaders and conspiracist arguments.[6] For example:

- In Nigeria, many people claim that the populist president Muhammadu Buhari actually died in 2017, but ever since, he has been impersonated by a Sudanese person.
- In India, Narendra Modi's government has claimed that Greta Thunberg, an ecologist activist, is part of a worldwide plot to denigrate his country's tea.
- In Russia, Vladimir Putin blamed a Western conspiracy to humiliate Russia by propagating "false" statistics about the numbers of covid-19 virus victims there.
- The former populist Brazilian leader President Jair Bolsonaro often advocated that environmental activists were the devious tool of foreign powers.
- Soon after the outbreak of Covid-19, the World Health Organization (WHO) coined the word "infoepidemic" to name the spread of conspiracies, images, and videos about the virus. One particularly blatant example of American conspiracy thinking is the video watched by more than eight million people across social media before it was removed. In it, Dr Anthony Fauci, a notable American contagious

disease authority, is falsely accused of making the virus and forwarding it to China.[7] The same video deceitfully claims that wearing masks will cause self-infection. President Trump fostered this and other conspiracies by refusing to wear a mask. Thousands of his followers followed his behaviour and an unknown number were infected by Covid-19 and possibly died as a result.

- In Canada, one of the top polling research firms concluded in 2022 that a significant percentage of Canadians hold opinions very similar to the politics of Donald Trump; for example, 52 per cent believe that official governmental information cannot be trusted and 37 per cent "think there is a group of people in this country who are trying to replace native-born Canadians with immigrants who agree with their political views."[8]

Conspiracy Theory: Definitions

Conspiracy theorizing is the public expression of gossip. It "is the belief that an organization made up of individuals or groups was or is acting covertly to achieve some malevolent end."[9] Conspiracy theories are "concerned about the struggle between good and evil, the conflict between villains acting in secret to manipulate the unsuspecting masses and the few who, having seen through their plot, are doing their upmost to thwart it."[10] At the heart of the theories is the urgent desire to explain evil. The assassination of President Kennedy is one of the most conspiracy-theorized happenings of recent times. Integral to this conspiracy theory is the assumption that the powers behind the murder have prevented their role being discovered.[11]

Throughout history significant political, economic, and cultural crises have encouraged conspiracy theories to emerge.[12] The theories seek to explain that these crises are caused by secretive, evil plots comprising many actors: a mysterious "them" who manipulate life against "us."[13] The theories then give "us" a reason to stigmatize and scapegoat "them." Hitler claimed that Jews were poisoning the German Aryan blood and Aryan soul, thus holding back Germany from becoming a dominant nation; they had to be eliminated. Many Germans unquestionably accepted this conspiracy theory (see Chapter 3).[14]

Four key qualities commonly characterize conspiracy theories: first, everything is controlled by design, and nothing is accidental;[15] second, "*Nothing is as it seems*,"[16] so appearances camouflage the actions of conspirators; and third, "*Everything is connected*"[17] (i.e. conspirators are actively ensuring, despite appearances to the contrary, that everything is planned to promote the evil results);[18] and fourthly, acceptance of a theory, as in magic, is ultimately an *act of faith* and not a judgement based on empirical proof (see Chapter 4).[19]

Types of Conspiracy Theories

Since the literature on conspiracy theories is vast and growing, it is helpful to divide them into types, and authors suggest different ways to categorize them.

- Barkum divides theories into three basic types: event conspiracies, systemic conspiracies, and superconspiracies.[20] An event conspiracy seeks to explain one incident, for example, the assassination of President Kennedy. In a systemic conspiracy, plotters are active in many events and over time; for example, Jews are blamed for all kinds of disasters over centuries. Behind a superconspiracy there is a vast complex of interconnected plotters actively joining their different conspiracies together to manipulate world events. Conspiracy theories are the motive power shaping the world, and virtually any institution may be suspected to be involved in some way or the other.
- Daniel Pipes divides theories into *petty conspiracy* and *world conspiracy* theories; the first involves fears about people wanting to acquire local advantage, while the latter claim that evil forces are actively seeking to control global affairs. However, I prefer simply to divide conspiracy theories into *local* and *global* theories.

Local Conspiracies

The conspiracy-inspired anti-Catholic and racist Know-Nothing Party flourished in the United States in the mid-nineteenth century. The Ku Klux Klan, a white supremacist sect, was founded as a terrorist movement, reaching its peak in the 1920s with over four million members. Their core conspiracy belief was to restore America to being a white, Christian nation free from drugs, homosexuality, immigration, and race-mixing, which the Klan believed caused (and continues to cause) the nation's decline. The Kennedy assassination generated a number of theories that seek to explain to Americans the hidden forces that caused this tragic event. Peter Knight, an authority on conspiracy cultures, comments: "The assassination and its accompanying culture of conspiracy never seem to be far from the headlines, nor from popular culture."[21]

In 1958, Robert Welch, a successful businessman, founded a highly influential right-wing political advocacy party, the John Birch Society. It was fuelled by a conspiracy theory that the American government, including the president, was part of a secret organization together with Soviet Russia to form a world government. Welch also scapegoated communists for placing fluoride in public water supplies.[22] He called for defending the police against accusations of police brutality and opposed using fluoride in the water supply. He claimed:

> [S]ocial change neither as a positive development for African Americans nor as a move toward a United States that more accurately reflected the constitutional principles of equality and freedom. Instead, progress toward a more just and equitable political community is understood to be the result of a Communist conspiracy.[23]

He claimed that President Eisenhower was encouraging the communists and that President Kennedy was a traitor. Welch and his fellow Birchers refused to accept the legitimacy of political adversaries, as would their Trumpite successors, claiming that whoever disagreed with them was acting in bad faith, if not as part of a malevolent conspiracy.

To understand the powerful influence of Birchers in their time, we need to recall the proposition: *whenever a culture or nation's power is under threat expect conspiracy theories to arise* (see *Proposition 10*, Chapter 1). The United States in the 1960s was experiencing cultural trauma, because its mythology of almost divinely ordered ongoing success was being gravely challenged by the breakdown of trust in government, the fear of communism, civil rights movement, and anti-Vietnam War protests. As James Patterson comments, "Confrontation, violence, and social disorder indeed seemed almost ubiquitous in America during the mid- and late 1960s."[24] Indeed, this was an ideal atmosphere for the John Birch Society to flourish.

The "America First" conspiracy theory effectively united Donald Trump with his supporters in 2017. It describes a nation that has lost its identity due to the polluting behaviour of immigrants, and elites who show more allegiance to global interests than to local needs. George Packer writes:

> America First is the conviction that the country has lost its traditional identity because of contamination and weakness – the contamination of others, foreigners, immigrants, Muslims; the weakness of elites who have no allegiance to the country because they've been globalized. . . . This narrative has contempt for democratic norms and liberal values, and it has an autocratic character. It personalizes power, routinizes corruption and destabilizes the very idea of objective truth.[25]

Implicit in this story is the promotion of the conspiracy theory that blames other people and events for assumed contemporary crises. This one insists on less federal government. I would also add a further violent quality to the theory, namely a policy of wildly denigrating and destroying the past in order to allow the secular nirvana to emerge.[26]

Global Theories

Examples of *global theories* are increasingly influential. For example, there is the widely popular Illuminati theory that claims there is a secret international organization consisting of the world's top political and social elite that control the workings of the entire world.[27] It began in eighteenth-century Bavaria and frequently reappears in different forms; for example, there are the many New World Order conspiracies, all claiming that a secret group is out to dominate the world. To prove that the Illuminati exists, believers point to symbols such as the Eye of Horus and pyramid openly displayed on US currency. When believers see such symbols in popular media, they immediately conclude that the organizers or institutions using them belong to the Illuminati.[28] Following the Second World War, the Illuminati were blamed for the rise of Nazism, fascism, and communism. Pat Robertson, an evangelist and media mogul, claimed that the Illuminati were responsible for undermining Christianity and American freedoms, prior to launching their criminally inspired government.[29]

Global anti-Catholic conspiracy theories have flourished for centuries. Some have claimed that Catholic groups have been involved in human sacrifice, Satanic actions, and black masses. Others accuse the Vatican for starting the two world wars, the rise of communism, Nazism, and even the assassinations of Abraham Lincoln and John F. Kennedy. Popular American fundamentalist and cartoonist Jack Chick (1924–2016) widely spread conspiracy theories that Catholics were not Christian and that the Vatican had created Islam to destroy other Christian churches and Jewish people.[30]

The Pizzagate theory emerged in late 2016. It claims that high officials of the Democratic party were involved in a child sex trafficking club residing in the basement of a pizza shop in Washington, DC. The theory became increasingly weird, finally claiming that an elite, Satanic, cannibalistic, child sex trafficking ring operated out of the Comet Ping Pong pizza parlour in the city. It asserted that John Podesta, Hillary Clinton's campaign manager, had ordered pizza from this parlour. The highly influential and baseless QAnon theory further expanded on Pizzagate. It started in October 2017 as an exclusively American conspiracy theory but it has spread, and continues to develop, in updated forms to other parts of the world.[31] Supporters claim that the Trump administration secretly struggled against a powerful cabal of people who control the world.[32] This evil group consists of Democratic politicians, Satan-worshipping paedophiles, and Hollywood celebrities who conduct a global child sex-trafficking ring, gathering the blood of children for life-sustaining chemicals. It is believed that Trump will conduct mass arrests and executions of thousands of followers on a day termed "the Storm" or "the Event."[33] Alex Jones (1974–), radio show host, further expanded QAnon by promulgating the theory that several governments and big businesses have plotted to form a "New World Order" by fostering economic crises, complex surveillance technology, and terrorism.

On May 30, 2019, the Federal Bureau of Investigation classified Pizzagate and QAnon as "fringe political" conspiracy theories, declaring that they likely motivate domestic extremists to commit violent and other criminal actions. It is no surprise, therefore, that many of those arrested for participating in the January 6, 2021, assault on the Capitol building were found to be supporters of the QAnon theory. *The Economist* reported early in 2021 that "Fully half of Mr Trump's supporters claimed to believe its core falsehoods: that he was fighting a high-level Democratic child-sex operation."[34] Trump and supporters have at least implicitly encouraged QAnon. For example, Marjorie Taylor Greene, a member of House of Representatives and avid promoter of QAnon, "has harnessed the paranoia inherent in conspiratorial thinking and reassured a significant a swath of voters that it is okay – no, righteous" to believe in the conspiracy theory. She "declared at a Michigan rally . . . 'Democrats want Republicans dead, and they've already started the killings.' Greene did not create this sensibility, but she channels it better than any of her colleagues."[35]

"Deep state" is a generalized conspiracy theory claiming that there is an unlawful state within a state, such as the Illuminati, consisting of secret and unauthorized networks of power with its own agenda and aims. The theory is an integral quality of QAnon. Democrats, the Hollywood elite, business tycoons, wealthy liberals, and others are under the authority of Barack Obama, a secret Muslim, and the murderer Hilary Clinton. They are financially supported by George Soros and the Rothschild banking family. Their aim is to destroy the American democratic way of life. But the mysterious Q will effectively prevent this from happening.[36] Eirikur Bergmann notes, "In a 2017 poll, *ABC News* and *The Washington Post* found that almost half of Americans believed in a conspiratorial *deep state* in the US."[37]

The Great Replacement conspiracy theory claims that there is an international Jewish conspiracy to move non-white people to traditionally white countries in an effort to "replace" whites with a more pliant, racially inferior population.[38] It continues to be spread globally through online message boards; Fox News's Tucker Carlson has uncritically referred to it on his show more than four hundred times.[39] Not surprisingly, the theory assumes that immigrants are part of a scheme to replace the political power and culture of white people residing in Western countries.

Political scientists Russell Muirhead and Nancy Rosenblum believe that an entirely new type of conspiracy theorizing has recently emerged, namely "conspiracy *without* the theory. And the new conspiracism betrays a new destructive impulse: to delegitimate democracy."[40] In the past theorists sought to give "proofs" of their theories, but now, the authors argue, there is little emphasis on evidence but instead on repetition: "no dots revealed to form a pattern, no close examination of the operators plotting in the shadows. . . . Instead, we have innuendo and verbal gesture: 'A lot of people are saying . . .' Or we have the assertion: 'Rigged!' – a one word exclamation."[41] So Trump and his supporters for the last four years have kept repeating over and over again that the presidential elections of November 3, 2020, were rigged, despite clear information to the contrary. And the repetition has worked.

Case Study: The Trump Experience

Conspiracy theories have spawned a veritable industry of books, tabloid articles, films, and television programmes, all of which are consumed with great enjoyment by great numbers of Americans. This is not surprising. They are particularly susceptible to conspiracy theories "due to its anti-government, apocalyptic religious and entrepreneurial traditions."[42] They will not disappear simply because the founding mythology of God-decreed success cannot allow the American nation to tolerate failure for any lengty period. Hence, conspiracy theories particularly flourish for Americans whenever their world moves from relative stability to widespread turmoil, with its accompanying uncertainties and fears.[43] There is a breakdown of trust in governments and other agencies to control what is happening, leaving the door wide open for conspiracy theories and populist leaders.[44] Trump tapped into the American tradition of conspiracy theorizing. His encouragement of conspiracy theories had a special appeal to his followers: the governmental elites and others are always up to something malevolent and they are trying to hide this.

Richard Hofstadter claimed in 1964, in his classic article "The Paranoid Style in American Politics," that American politics have been influenced by conspiracy theories particularly since the Kennedy presidency,[45] but with the coming of the Trump administration, such theories became politically normalized. Hofstadter argues that conspiracy thinkers feel a profound sense of persecution, which they categorize into "grandiose theories of conspiracy."[46] He distinguishes between the "clinical paranoiac" and the "paranoid political spokesman." While they share some qualities such as being "overheated, oversuspicious, overaggressive, grandiose, and apocalyptic in expression," they significantly differ. In particular, Hofstadter writes, clinical paranoiacs believe threats are focused on them, but political paranoiacs claim the threats are directed against a nation, culture, and style of living.[47] Consequently, political paranoiacs are so firmly convinced of their own altruistic and patriotic motives that they have a sense of "righteousness and moral indignation."[48] "What Marjorie Taylor Greene has accomplished is this. She has harnessed the paranoia inherent in conspiratorial thinking and reassured a significant swarth of voters that it is okay – no, righteous – to indulge their suspicions about the left, the Republican establishment, the media."[49]

During Trump's presidency hardly a day passed without a new charge of conspiracy, from "fake news" to "rigged elections."[50] Seeking the presidency in 2016, he wooed his followers with conspiracy theories that responded to the needs of people, particularly "working class whites in the Midwest, who felt ill-served by both major parties and could conceive of no benign explanation for social and economic changes that angered and dismayed them."[51] And in his narratives conspiring foreign governments outsmarted a selfish political elite in Washington. When Trump began to campaign with the catchcry "Make America Great Again," xenophobic right-wing populism reached a new level of vicious cultic fundamentalism in the United States.[52] As a populist leader, Trump became a "rage machine,"[53] hitting out at whatever his followers felt angry and resentful about.[54] He demanded a "total and complete shutdown" of America's borders to Muslim migrants and visitors, proposing to deport eleven million undocumented immigrants *en masse*, building a wall along the Mexican-American border to be paid for by the Mexican government. In addition to using derogatory words of women, he "referred to Mexicans crossing the border as rapists; called enthusiastically for the use of torture . . .; advocated killing the families of terrorists."[55] The more offensive and xenophobic he became, the more his widespread following increased.

No one was spared Trump's abuse; even President Obama was accused of having no legitimate American birth certificate.[56] He had little respect, and to some degree, outright antipathy, for his party's leaders.[57] And his followers could not get enough of his unrestrained conspiracy accusations and anger. All the time he returned to the founding experience of the nation, the civic mythological belief that God destines America to be great and his task was to make it great again! Trump based his re-election campaign in 2020 on several different conspiracy narratives, for example blaming the rapid spread of Covid-19 in the United States on China and WHO. The consequence of Trump's support for conspiracy theories, his frequent stream of small lies, and his false claim that the last presidential elections were rigged helped to further undermine people's respect for truth.[58] Be assured! When Trump and his followers move off centre stage, others will take their place with new and possibly more outlandish conspiracy theories.

There is a further feature in the founding mythology of the United States that populist leaders like Trump tap into: the lone super-hero cowboy and the west so well portrayed in the *Lone Ranger* films in earlier days. The Lone Ranger in the frontier west would gallop ahead to solve an injustice that government officials ignore, thus rescuing the oppressed from the impasse of cultural trauma; having succeeded, he would again gallop west into the lonely evening ready to respond successfully to yet another injustice most likely caused by a corrupt government official.[59] In later American Western films, as in *Shane* (1953) or *Cat Ballou* (1965), the hero is also a strong, self-contained individual unknown to or not fully accepted by society, who possesses exceptional abilities which he uses successfully to defend a powerless society against the evil actions of the villain. The society finally accepts the saviour it had earlier rejected. The cowboy hero of Western films has now been modernized through the *Rocky* and *Rambo* films of Sylvester Stallone and in, more recent times, the *Terminator* films of Arnold Schwarzenegger and Bruce Willis' defeating successive sets of terrorists in *Die Hard* (1988), *Die Harder* (1990), and *Die Hard: With a Vengeance* (1995). The vigorously individualistic, macho, physically strong, thoroughly self-contained, and silent person, the "truly American" hero is centre stage once more, destroying villains with modern firepower, using helicopters in place of horses, restoring the morale of the American people, prepared to return at any time when needed to uphold the American way of life. The individual hero will always return the people to a journey of success because governments are believed to be too weak or corrupt.[60]

Why Do Conspiracy Theories Flourish?

Proposition 1: Conspiracy theories are stories supplying meaning in cultural crises.

A fundamental anthropological truth in this book is that "one can neither work nor play nor theorize with chaos. Pure chaos is pure terror. One must find forms and frames within which to contain it."[61] A culture is held together by stories, that is, myths that people tell one another. These myths are "webs of significance,"[62] because they give meaning and identity to people. When cultures disintegrate these myths fail to function. Cultures fall into the dreaded chaos. Conspiracy beliefs arise that satisfy people's needs for certainty, security, and a positive self-image in a world that they feel is falling apart. Then paranoia makes sense.[63] Little wonder that conspiracies globally continue to flourish following the cultural traumas of the 2008 financial crisis and Covid-19. They are stories that offer an artificial simplification of the vast unknowable forces that people feel are manipulating national and global societies; they respond to a real need for persons and cultures that cannot maintain their self-esteem unless they perceive themselves to be victims of intrigue.[64] Peter Knight writes that Americans are particularly susceptible to conspiracy beliefs because for them their world has moved from relative stability to widespread turmoil with its accompanying uncertainties and fears. There is a breakdown of trust in governments and other agencies to control what is happening, leaving the door wide open for global conspiracy theories.[65]

An inability to live with uncertainty and ambiguity draws people to conspiracy theories when they validate their apprehensions. One story answers all their fears. Thus, the anarchists who invaded the Capitol in Washington in 2021 stormed the buildings with absolute certitude that the elections had been rigged. Michael Butter concludes that the overwhelming amount of research finds that gender, age, and socio-economic status have little or no impact on belief in conspiracy theories: "While some studies find that men are more likely to believe in them, others come to the exact opposite result, and most find no difference."[66]

Muirhead and Rosenblum alert readers to the findings of an increasing number of cognitive and social psychologists that it is quite normal for people's mental processes to have a bias towards believing that powerful hidden forces are actively controlling events. Devotees of conspiracy theories may not necessarily be abnormal. Cognitively the human mind looks for clear-cut patterns in events. Nothing is accidental. This bias in thinking is called *intentionality*. The second cognitive quality is *proportionality*. When something significant happens to us we expect to find a cause equal to the event, however outlandish it may be.[67]

Proposition 2: Conspiracy theories give people a feeling of belonging to a valued community.

Conspiracy theories will always be popular, because they make people feel smart, important, and part of a community at times when people feel lost and unvalued.[68]

Proposition 3: Conspiracy theories flourish wherever trust in cultures breaks down, for example, when institutions in their decision-making processes remain secretive, thus fostering distrust.[69]

Trust is "a relationship between one or more persons, which has elements of openness and honesty, and a willingness to accept others based on the opinion that the other party is both capable and dependable."[70] Charles Feltman describes trust as "choosing to risk making something you value vulnerable to another person's actions." And distrust is deciding that "what is important to me is not safe with this person in this situation (or any situation)."[71] No organizational culture can maintain morale if trust in its leaders disintegrates. A community's culture is said to be trusting when there is a kind of collective judgement that the people involved will act with honesty in negotiations, and make "a good faith effort to behave in accordance with [their] commitments."[72] Where trust exists, people feel valued and levels of job satisfaction are increased.[73] When trust crumbles fear takes its place. Katherine Hawley perceptively highlights the centrality of trust in the maintenance of any community: "Trust is at the centre of a whole web of concepts: reliability, predictability, expectation, cooperation, goodwill, and – on the dark side – distrust, insincerity, conspiracy, betrayal, and incompetence."[74] When basic trust of members of a group is broken, it is in danger of becoming perverted and replaced by the *blind* or *unquestioning trust* characteristic of fundamentalist movements and believers in conspiracy theories.[75] For example, when Pope John Paul I died suddenly in 1978, the Vatican Press Office reported that he had been found with *The Imitation of Christ* in his hand. This was incorrect, but the story was "touched up, sanitized, made more edifying for public consumption."[76] Little wonder that his death encouraged conspiracy theories.

In conspiracies truth and objectivity lose out. As long as the group is protected from the assumed source of evil, nothing else is important, no matter what moral or physical violence the innocent experience. The preservation or the restoration of the status quo must be achieved at all costs.[77] But the difference between the past and the present is that conspiracy theorizing has moved from the fringes of societies into mainstream life, so much so that democracies worldwide are under threat.[78] Today conspiracy theories such as QAnon threaten the very existence of democratic governments because they make people feel helpless, thus opening the way for authoritarian regimes to flourish. At the end of his study of the John Birch Society, Edward Miller warns of the dangers to all democracies from conspiracy theories. "The conspiratorial style threatens democracy because it poisons the mind and makes it difficult to see reality. It allows people to be led in dark directions, even when their actions are contrary to the better angels of their characters."[79]

Trust includes an expectation of honesty, the assumption that others will do their best to meet their commitments, because they have the appropriate knowledge, skill, or ability.[80] Lying, writes Sissela Bok, is "any intentionally deceptive message."[81] Truthfulness in communication demands, first, avoiding lies and deceiving people directly and intentionally. Otherwise, communication becomes a violent manipulation of people. Truthfulness, however, is much more than not telling lies or deceiving; it necessitates disclosing information to those who have a right to it.[82] Not lying is the ethical sine qua non of any human communication; to knowingly create or foster conspiracy beliefs is to falsify truth.[83]

Conspiracy Theories Cause Harm

Conspiracy theories are ubiquitous and cause immense harm to people, influencing political policy decisions and social behaviours, including medical choices. Sociologist Michael Butter lists three foremost ways why conspiracy theories were particularly dangerous during the Covid-19 pandemic: they could "lead to radicalization and violence; they can make people disregard medical knowledge and, as a consequence, endanger themselves and others; and they can undermine trust in elected politicians and the democratic process as such."[84] Vulnerable peoples, such as immigrants, minority groups, and people who are poor, were in constant danger of being wrongfully blamed, stigmatized, and further marginalized for falsely causing the virus and its consequences (see Chapter 3).

In Norway, in 2011, Anders Behring Breivik massacred seventy-seven people because he believed in the conspiracy theory that Europe was being destroyed by the mass immigration of Muslims. He accused feminists and the social democratic elite of deceiving people by fostering the evil of multiculturalism.[85] In 2019 in New Zealand forty-nine people were massacred by an anti-Muslim terrorist. In Australia, 2022, three people were gunned down by three terrorists motivated by the fundamentalist conspiracy theory of Christian premillennialism.[86] In India the Muslim minority became a scapegoat for Covid-19.[87] In Holland, lockdown restrictions to control Covid-19 evoked destructive riots. Many protestors endorsed conspiracy theories that assumed the government had nefarious motives, such as exaggerating the perils of the virus to suppress the people or imposing forced vaccinations with mysterious substances that facilitate mind control.[88] Likewise, anti-vaccine conspiracy theories in the United States and elsewhere poisoned the minds and endangered the bodies of many citizens. Consequently the vaccination rate slowed down.[89]

Unscrupulous and power-driven leaders can exploit people's needs for conspiracy thinking in times of cultural crises. Likewise, unprincipled followers can support these populist leaders and their conspiracy theories for their own advantage. Thus, Republicans backed McCarthy and his anti-Communist craze, "because his success in dramatizing the Communist issue was also a way of discrediting the New Deal and the Truman administration."[90] Today the belief that President Joseph Biden stole the presidential election from Donald Trump has been actively promoted or quietly acquiesced to by most Republican political leaders.[91] Jonathan Rauch warns:

> Blame Trump and his troll army and media enablers . . . but remember that they could not have succeeded without their audience's help. Disinformation and conspiracism spread in advanced, individualistic democracies . . . not because their targets are sheeplike but because to the contrary, so many people are active collaborators in their own deception. . . . Feeling that their voices and votes are disregarded . . . they search for a narrative which offers a heroic role in a millenarian drama.[92]

Responding to Conspiracy Theories

Conspiracy theorizing is one of the most problematic subjects for concerned people to expose calmly and thoughtfully. Conspiracy devotees apply so much emotional energy to their conspiracy theories that it is nearly impossible to keep track of what they are saying and to question their beliefs.[93]

Guideline 1: Efforts to dialogue with ideological conspiracy theorists have doubtful results.

Possibly the best argument against conspiracy theories is that they are entrenched in an assumption of human behaviour and history that contradict the findings of social sciences. Conspiracy theorists falsely assume that we are able to control the development of human history for years, even decades, "according to [our] own intentions – in other words, that history is plannable."[94] Although a dialogue is theoretically possible with theorists, it will not usually have the desired effect: "To challenge the theory is to shatter the self-image of the person . . . This may be gratifying for the challenger, but it serves little purpose beyond that of self-affirmation."[95] Convinced believers in witchcraft, sorcery, and conspiracy theories are not impressed by scientific arguments.[96] As they provide their committed devotees with a much-needed mythological sense of identity and security in the midst of chaos, they are not easily discredited by rational presentation of facts (see Chapter 4).[97] Presenting believers with the proven empirical evidence contrary to the theory in fact often further reinforces their belief: "Conspiracy theories are generally designed by circular reasoning: both evidence for it are misinterpreted as evidence of its truth, whereby the conspiracy becomes a matter of faith rather than something that can be proven or disproven."[98]

"Ideology" is a highly contested word.[99] However, in the context of conspiracy thinkers ideology is an action-oriented, rigid, and dramatic understanding of the person and the world. It is "the distortion of truth for the sake of collective interests."[100] A person or culture is emotionally and entirely controlled by an ideology, and it becomes for the people involved a dogmatic faith which can in no way be questioned. Ideologists *pre*-judge everything according to this dogmatic assertion and they will not listen to any argument that in any way throws doubt on the truth of the pre-judgement. For example, a committed conspiracist will see evil in every person or group that does not think or believe as they do.

Pontius Pilate claimed to be an open Roman ruler, a so-called liberal thinker, but he was in fact also a vigorous ideologist. "Pilate asked him, 'What is truth?'" "After he had said this, he went out to the Jews again" (John 18:38). He was so committed to the view that no objective, unchanging truth can exist that he refused to listen to any opinion to the contrary. He asked his question of Jesus, but immediately rushed off to avoid hearing the answer.[101] The truth Pilate did not want to hear was the revelation that Christ brings from the Father, the revelation that God loves us and that we are called to love our neighbours as ourselves.

Guideline 2: It is possible to dialogue with doubting conspiracy theorists.

Doubting theorists are not fully convinced of a conspiracy theory. If people are not *entirely* convinced of a theory there is a greater chance that they will accept that the theory lacks objective truth. A sensitive approach is required; people need to be listened to and invited to give the sources of a conspiracy theory. In a calm atmosphere the challenger is then able to show that a theory has no foundation in reality.

The challenger needs gifts of listening and dialogue. Dialogue is that "address and response between persons in which there is a flow of meaning between them in spite of all the obstacles that normally would block the relationship."[102] It is that interaction between people in which each aims to give themselves as they are and seeks also to know the other as the other is. Dialogue is authentic, therefore, if three conditions are met: people feel they understand the position of others; they also feel that others understand their points of view; and there is a readiness on the part of all to accept what is decided because it was reached openly and fairly. The capacity to listen places people in contact with the wider dimensions of the world in which they live. Authentic listening is able to break through the rigid borders that imprison fundamentalist thinking; this allows people to engage with the world beyond. In most attempted dialogues "we don't listen; we just reload."[103] Patience and creativity are required in great measure to win through the walls of intolerance.

Guideline 3: Value the findings of the social sciences.

The more people are educated in the analytical skills of the social sciences, for example, anthropology, sociology, and psychology, the more critical they can become of conspiracy theories in the media and elsewhere.[104] By understanding why people succumb to conspiracies and how they are sustained, we can be educated to think more critically about unverified conspiracy theories.

Scriptural Critique

Faith in Christ Redeemer is the ultimate source of our identity, not an ideological and untrue belief contained in a conspiracy theory. When

Jesus speaks about faith, it is usually the kind necessary for salvation and healing. Thus he commended the faith of the woman cured of bleeding (Luke 8:48), the man cured of blindness (Luke 18:42), and the grateful Samaritan leper who returned to praise God (Luke 17:19). Those who demonstrate such faith are named as "saved." They believed in Christ not primarily because he was a physical healer but because he gave them faith in himself. Jesus asked the gratefully healed leper: "Were there not ten made clean? But the other nine, where are they?" (Luke 17:19). The nine were closed to the gift of faith because they were ideologically blinded by their refusal to see beyond their bodily healing.

Truth-telling: a Scriptural imperative.

> One who secretly slanders a neighbour I will destroy . . .
> No one who practices deceit shall remain in my house; no one who utters lies shall continue in my presence.
>
> (Ps 101: 5, 7)

In the Scriptures, truthfulness is listed among the premier values. History is a battle between divine Truth and Satan and his followers. In the Old Testament the commandment "You shall not bear false witness against your neighbour" (Exod 20:16) defends God's people from evil and harmful untruths and infidelities. Lying violently opposes the covenant that unites the people of God and evokes fidelity and reliability. The thankful reaction to the gift of the covenant is fidelity and truthfulness before God and towards each other.

The lamentation psalms are dramatic rituals of truth-telling.[105] The Israelites are confronted with overpowering evils such as their alienation from God through sinfulness, sickness, and exile from their beloved temple and country. They feel utterly wretched, which they can no longer hide from themselves and God. Because they are united in one covenant with God, they believe that they have every right to let God know what they feel about their sufferings and how God will be obligated to do something about them. Ponder the public lament of the Israelites as they agonizingly view the destruction of the temple, the most pivotal symbol of God's presence in their midst. Desolation reigns supreme. Once their sadness is dramatically proclaimed and put aside, the Israelites discover space within their hearts for hopeful trust in God:

> O God, why do you cast us off forever. . . . Your foes have roared within your holy place . . . with hatchets and hammers, they smashed all its carved work. . . . Rise up, O God, plead your cause, remember how the impious scoff at you all the day long.
>
> (Ps 74:1, 4, 6, 22)

The New Testament tells the believer that Jesus Christ is "the Covenant and Faithful Witness" and "the believer shares in his saving truth and his mission to give faithful witness; the liar can have no share in this covenant."[106] Bernard Haring further comments: "As a basic normative ideal, the New Testament stresses the striving for exemplary truthfulness and trustworthiness (Matt 5:37). All kinds of lying damage that the community and credibility must be cast aside as the old self, the sinner (Eph 4:25; Col 3:9)."[107] Ananias and Sapphira, who purposely deceived their faith community and introduced an attitude of hypocrisy, were sternly punished (Acts 5:1-11). Ananias and his wife, Sapphira, freely and publicly agreed to pool all their goods for the benefit of the young Christian community, but they secretly held back some for themselves. Peter discovered the deception. To Ananias he said: "How is it that you contrived this deed in your heart? You did not lie to us but to God!" (Acts 5:4). And to Sapphira: "How is it that you have agreed together to put the Spirit of the Lord to the test?" (Acts 5:9). The seriousness of fraud and lying by Ananias and Sapphira, punished by their death, evoked great fear in "the whole church and all who heard of these things" (Acts 5:11).

St Peter warns his readers against leaders who aim to exploit their fears. He writes to reassure Christians whose faith has been disturbed because the predictions of the Parousia have not been confirmed.[108] They must carefully assess the credentials of leaders before accepting what they are saying: "But false prophets also arose among the people, just as there will be false teachers among you, who secretly bring in destructive opinions" (2 Pet 2:1). The same wisdom is needed today lest deceitful people twist reality by their conspiracy theories to suit their malicious intentions.

Faith calls us to be open to truth no matter its origin.

Despite the often evil qualities of conspiracy theorizing, there may be something we can learn from them and the people who support them. At times Christ criticizes Pharisees; nonetheless, he reminds the disciples that there are positive points in their behaviour towards himself: they caution Jesus that Herod endangers his life (Luke 13:31); they invite him for meals (Luke 7:36–50; 14:1); Jesus admires their zeal (Matt 23: 15) and their concern for perfection and purity (Matt 5: 20); they shelter early Christians (Acts 5:34; 23: 6-9). Certain church Fathers, such as Justin, Irenaeus, and Clement of Alexandria, either explicitly or in an equivalent manner, speak about the "seeds" sown by the Word of God in cultures.[109] Justin claims: "Everything good that has been said, no matter by whom, is Christian."[110] And St Thomas Aquinas often wrote, "If something is true, no matter who said it, it is always from the Holy Spirit."[111]

The Word of God is actively present, although in an incomplete way, in all cultures and peoples. This presence or glimmer of the transcendence is the foreshadowing of the fuller revelation of Jesus Christ in the Scriptures and tradition. Whatever is good, however small it may be, in the behaviour of people comes from the Spirit.[112] As Karl Rahner writes, "the very commonness of everyday things harbours the eternal marvel and silent mystery of God and [God's] grace."[113] St John Paul II describes this mystery in these words: "Lying deep in every culture, there appears this impulse towards a fulfilment. We may say, then, that culture itself has an intrinsic capacity to receive divine Revelation."[114] Faith in Christ thus tells us that the Holy Spirit is the source of all truth, no matter where it is found. Hence, even in the midst of the negativities of conspiracy theories, the Holy Spirit is inviting us to be open to what is troubling conspiracy believers.

Summary Points

- A conspiracy theory is "the belief that an organization made up of individuals or groups was or is acting covertly to achieve some malevolent end."[115] As with gossip a theory seeks to explain evil.
- Local and global conspiracy theories flourish at times of cultural, economic, and political chaos. They are able to resolve a human need for making sense of a chaotic situation.
- They can be used by unscrupulous leaders to gain and maintain power. For example, Hitler claimed that Jews were poisoning the German Aryan blood and Aryan soul, thus holding back Germany from becoming a dominant nation; they had to be eliminated.[116]
- Conspiracy theories are unverifiable truths. Since people *believe* conspiracy theories, it is usually impossible to undermine them with objective factual information. This is further explained in Chapter 4.
- The scriptures call Christians to be truth-tellers in imitation of Christ who is "the way, the truth, and the life" (John 14:6).

Discussion Questions

1. Because we are surrounded by conspiracy theories, am I at least unconsciously believing in them?
2. What is lacking in people's lives that makes them support these theories?
3. Why do conspiracy thinkers tolerate the violence their theories can cause?
4. "Jesus said to [Thomas] 'I am the way, the truth, and the life. No one comes to the Father except through me'" (John 14:6). What are the implications of this text for the followers of Christ?

Notes

1. Conspiracy theories occur in all societies, but the term "conspiracy theory" was first used by Karl Popper in 1945, *The High Tide of Prophecy: Hegel, Marx, and the Aftermath* (London: Routledge & Kegan Paul, 1945), 94.
2. Michael Barkum, *A Culture of Conspiracy: Apocalyptic Visions in Contemporary America* (Berkeley, CA: University of California Press, 2013), 7.
3. James Mann, "The Birchers and the Trumpers," *The New York Review of Books* (June 23, 2022), 37.
4. Adrienne LaFrance, "The New Anarchy," *The Atlantic* (April, 2023), 37.
5. Jonathan Swift quoted in "From Congo to the Capitol, Conspiracy Theories Are Surging," *The Economist* (September 3, 2021), 18.
6. See Michael Butter, *The Nature of Conspiracy Theories* (Oxford: Polity, 2020), 7.
7. See World Health Organization, "Immunizing the Public Against Misinformation," www.who.int/news-room/feature-stories/detail/immunizing-the-public-against-misformation (Accessed September 20, 2020); "Fake News: Return of the Paranoid Style," *The Economist* (June 6, 2020), 50–1.
8. Keith Baldrey, "Rise of Conspiracy Theories Shows Canada Not Immune From U.S. Problems," htttps://globalnews.ca/news/8957657/rise-of-conspiracy-theories-shows-canada-not-immune-from-u-s-problems. (Accessed November 9, 2022).
9. Barkun, *A Culture of Conspiracy*, 3.
10. Butter, *The Nature of Conspiracy Theories*, 2.
11. See Peter Knight, *Conspiracy Culture: From Kennedy to the X-Files* (London: Routledge, 2000), 87–91.
12. See Rob Brotherton, *Suspicious Minds: Why We Believe Conspiracy Theories* (New York: Bloomsbury Sigma, 2015).
13. See Knight, *Conspiracy Culture*, 4.
14. Adolf Hitler stated 1922: "We in Germany have come to this: that sixty-million people see its destiny lie at the will of a few dozen Jewish bankers. . . . No salvation is possible until the bearer of disunion, the Jew, has been rendered powerless to harm." See Adolf Hitler, *My New Order* (New York: Reynal and Hitchcock, 1941), 45.
15. See Barkum, *A Culture of Conspiracy*, 3.
16. Barkum, *A Culture of Conspiracy*, 4. Italics in original.
17. Barkum, *A Culture of Conspiracy*, 4. Italics in original.
18. See Barkum, *A Culture of Conspiracy*, 4.
19. See Barkum, *A Culture of Conspiracy*, 7 and Martha F. Lee, *Conspiracy Rising: Conspiracy Thinking and American Public Life* (Santa Barbara, CA: Praeger, 2011), 6–7.
20. See Barkum, *A Culture of Conspiracy*, 6.
21. See Knight, *Conspiracy Culture*, 77.
22. See Edward H. Miller, *A Conspiratorial Life: Robert Welch, The John Birch Society, and the Revolution of American Conservatism* (Chicago: University of Chicago Press, 2021).

23 Lee, *Conspiracy Rising*, 76–7.
24 James T. Patterson, *Grand Expectations: The United States, 1945–74* (Oxford: Oxford University Press, 1997), 449.
25 George Packer, quoted in David Brooks, op-ed, "The Four American Narratives," *The New York Times* (May 26, 2017) (PDF).
26 There is conspiracy theory online which claims that bitcoin was invented by the US National Security Agency that is involved in cryptography research, though the actual origin of bitcoin is well known. See "Conspiracy Theories: Goldfingers?" *The Economist* (October 7, 2023), 69.
27 Information about the Illuminate is readily available in conspiracy sections of the YouTube and on websites such as www.illuminatiofficial.org. I first stumbled on the theory in the mid-1970s when a group of well-educated people sought to convince me unsuccessfully that the Illuminati existed. Nothing I said undermined their belief in the conspiracy.
28 See Barkum, *A Culture of Conspiracy*, 45–63.
29 See Patrick Robertson, *The New World Order* (Dallas: W Publishing Group, 1991); Eirikur Bergmann, *Conspiracy and Populism: The Politics of Misinformation* (Oxford: Palgrave, 2018), 25–8.
30 See Bergmann, *Conspiracy and Populism*, 30–1.
31 See Amy Gunia, "The US Exported QAnon to Australia and New Zealand," *Time* (September 30, 2020) (PDF).
32 See "It's All Connected, Man: From Congo to the Capitol, Conspiracy Theories Are Surging," *The Economist* (September 4, 2021), 45.
33 See Mike Rothschild, *The Storm Is Upon Us: How QAnon Became a Movement, Cult, and Conspiracy Theory of Everything* (London: Melville House, 2021); Adrienne LaFrance, "The Prophecies of Q," *The Atlantic* (May 14, 2020) (PDF).
34 "QAnon and Other Delusions," *The Economist* (January 30, 2021), 32.
35 Elaina Plott Calabro, "Why Is She Like This? On the Ground in Marjorie Taylor Greene's Alternate Universe," *The Atlantic* (January–February, 2023), 56.
36 See Rothschild, *The Storm Is Upon Us*, 11–12.
37 Eirikur Bergmann, *Conspiracy and Populism: The Politics of Misinformation* (Oxford: Palgrave, 2018), 34.
38 See "What Is the 'Great Replacement' Right-Wing Conspiracy Theory? Why Has It Spread to Mainstream Politics?" *The Economist* (May 16, 2022), 28.
39 See Steve Rose, "A Deadly Ideology: How the 'Great Replacement Theory' Went Mainstream," *The Guardian* (June 8, 2022) (PDF).
40 Russell Muirhead and Nancy L. Rosenblum, *A Lot of People Are Saying: The New Conspiracism and the Assault on Democracy* (Princeton: Princeton University Press, 2019), 2.
41 Muirhead and Rosenblum, *A Lot of People Are Saying*, 3.
42 "QAnon and Other Delusions," *The Economist*, 32.

43 See Arbuckle, *Fundamentalism at Home and Abroad: Analysis and Pastoral Responses* (Collegeville, MN: Liturgical Press, 2017), 11–12, 16–17; Martha F. Lee, *Conspiracy Rising: Conspiracy Thinking and American Public Life* (San Barbara: Praeger, 2011), 43–68. Daniel Hellinger notes that "Much of the power of post-War conspiracism in popular culture can be traced to anxieties about the loss of individualism." "Paranoia, Conspiracy, and Hegemony in American Politics," eds. Harry G. West and Todd Sanders, *Transparency and Conspiracy: Ethnographies of Suspicion in the New World Order* (Durham: Duke University Press, 2003), 219.
44 See Knight, *Conspiracy Culture*, 4, 242–4.
45 See Richard Hofstadter, *The Paranoid Style in American Politics and Other Essays* (New York: Knopf, 1965).
46 Richard Hofstadter, "The Paranoid Style in American Politics," *The Paranoid Style in American Politics, and Other Essays* (New York: Alfred A. Knopf, 1966), 4.
47 See Hofstadter, "The Paranoid Style in American Politics," 3–4.
48 Hofstadter, "The Paranoid Style in American Politics," 4.
49 Calabro, "Why Is She Like This?" 56.
50 See Muirhead and Rosenblum, *A Lot of People Are Saying*, 42–58.
51 "Lexington: Winning by Breaking – Donald Trump's Most Damaging Legacy May Be a Lower-Trust America," *The Economist* (December 24, 2016), 50.
52 See "Michael Flynn's Flying Circus: Part of Donald Trump's Base Thinks He Is Fighting a Spiritual War," *The Economist* (October 21, 2023), 33.
53 See Michael Tomasky, "Trump," *The New York Review of Books*, www.nybooks.com/articles/2015/09/24/trump/?utm_medium=email&utm_cam (Accessed December 14, 2015).
54 Carol Anderson comments: "Some 20 percent of Trump's supporters believed the Emancipation Proclamation had been bad public policy and that the enslaved should never have been freed." *White Rage: The Unspoken Truth of Our Racial Divide* (New York: Bloomsbury, 2017), 170–1. Anderson is quoting a survey by Libby Nelson, "Nearly 20 Percent of Trump's Supporters Disapprove of Lincoln Freeing the Slaves," *Vox* (February 24, 2016). (PDF).
55 "Trump Rages," *The Economist* (February 27, 2016), 9.
56 In July 2010, a CNN poll discovered that "Forty-two percent of those questioned say they have absolutely no doubts that the president was born in the U.S., while 29-percent say he 'probably' was." "CNN Poll: Quarter Doubt That Obama Born in US" (August 8, 2010) (PDF).
57 See Gerald Seib, "Trump Turning Republican Party Inside Out," *Wall Street Journal*, recorded by *The Australian* (February 24, 2016), 9.
58 See "Lexington: Republican Delusion About the Capitol Riot Hits a Dangerous New Low," *The Economist* (July 28, 2021), 49.

59 Daniel Boone, the great champion of the American frontier, became "a psychological repository of American virtues of courage, martial spirit, fierce individual autonomy, defiance of authority, and near-mystical combinations of continuous movement, pervasive entitlement, and dynamic achievement." Robert Jay Lifton, *The Protean Self: Human Resilience in an Age of Fragmentation* (New York: Basic Books, 1993), 35.
60 See Gerald A. Arbuckle, *Fundamentalism at Home and Abroad: Analysis and Pastoral Responses* (Collegeville, MN: Liturgical Press, 2017), 83–93.
61 C. Gareth Alford, "The Group as a Whole or Acting Out the Missing Leader," *International Journal of Group Psychotherapy*, vol. 45, no. 1 (1995): 133.
62 Clifford Geertz, *The Interpretation of Cultures* (New York: Basic Books, 1973), 5.
63 See Hofstadter, *The Paranoid Style*, 3–40; "How Paranoid Nationalism Corrupts" and "Looters With Flags," *The Economist* (September 2, 2023), 10, 18–20.
64 See Hans Toch, *The Social Psychology of Social Movements* (London: Methuen, 1965), 45–70.
65 See Knight, *Conspiracy Culture*, 4, 242–4.
66 Butter, *The Nature of Conspiracy Theories*, 74.
67 See Muirhead and Rosenblum, *A Lot of People Are Saying*, 45, 46.
68 See Mike Rothschild, *The Storm Is Upon Us*, 241–51; Karen M. Douglas, "COVID-19 Conspiracy Theories," *Sage Journals*, vol. 24, no. 2 (2021). (PDF).
69 See Knight, *Conspiracy Culture*, 28–32.
70 Rocky J. Dwyer, "Benchmarking as a Process for Demonstrating Organizational Trustworthiness?" *Management Decision*, vol. 46, no. 8 (2008): 1211–12.
71 Charles Feltman cited by Brene Brown, *Braving the Wilderness: The Quest for True Belonging and the Courage to Stand Alone* (London: Vermilion, 2017), 38.
72 Dwyer, "Benchmarking as a Process," 1212. An interesting example of what happens when trust in government breaks down comes from contemporary United States. In a Pew poll, it was found that only 19 per cent of Americans feel they can trust the government always or most of the time. "This erosion of trust eventually will limit the effectiveness of American government; indeed, in many ways it already has." Tyler Cowen, *The Complacent Class: The Self-Defeating Quest for the American Dream* (New York: St Martin's Press, 2017), 191.
73 See John Rodwell, Andrew Noblet, Defne Demir, and Peter Steane, "The Impact of the Work Conditions of Allied Health Professionals on Satisfaction, Commitment and Psychological Distress," *Health Care Management Review*, vol. 34, no. 3 (2009): 205–93.
74 Katherine Hawley, *Trust* (Oxford: Oxford University Press, 2012), 3.

75 See Vamik Volkan, *Blind Trust: Large Groups and Their Leaders in Times of Crisis and Terror* (Charlottesville: Pitchstone, 2004), 14.
76 Peter Hebblethwaite, *In the Vatican* (Oxford: Oxford University Press, 1986), 182.
77 See Gerald A. Arbuckle, *Violence, Society, and the Church: A Cultural Approach* (Collegeville, MN: Liturgical Press, 2004), 140–1.
78 See "It's All Connected, Man: From Congo to the Capitol, Conspiracy Theories are Surging," *The Economist* (September 4, 2021), 45–6; Gideon Rachman, *The Age of the Strong Man: How the Cult of the Leader Threatens Democracy around the World* (London: The Bodley Head, 2021), 1–24.
79 Miller, *A Conspiratorial Life*, 383.
80 See Katherine Hawley, *Trust* (Oxford: Oxford University Press, 2012), 48.
81 Sissela Bok, *Lying: Moral Choice in Public and Private Life* (Hassocks: Harvester Press, 1978), 13.
82 See Bernard Hoose, "Truth and Lies," ed. Bernard Hoose, *Christian Ethics: An Introduction* (Collegeville, MN: Liturgical Press, 1998), 266–76.
83 See James F. Keenan, *Ethics of the Word* (Lanham: Sheed and Ward, 2010), 115–19.
84 Butter, *The Nature of Conspiracy Theories*, 152.
85 See Eirikur Bergmann, *Conspiracy and Populism: The Politics of Misinformation* (Oxford: Palgrave, 2018), 1–3.
86 See Cloe Read, "Police Classify Train Murders as Terrorists," *The Sunday Morning Herald* (February 17, 2023), 23. Premillennialism is the belief that after a time of severe earthly hardship, Jesus Christ will bodily return and will reign for a thousand years bringing peace and prosperity.
87 See "Covid-19 and Autocracy," *The Economist* (April 25, 2020), 50.
88 See Jan-Willem van Prooijen, "Conspiracy Thinking: A Scapegoat Is Always Useful," *The Unesco Courier* (2021–2) (PDF) (Accessed July 27, 2021).
89 See "Lexington: The Anti-Vax Delusion," *The Economist* (July 17, 2021), 34; Gerald A. Arbuckle, *The Pandemic and the People of God: Cultural Impacts and Pastoral Responses* (Maryknoll, NY: Orbis Books, 2021), xv, 21.
90 Ted Morgan, *Reds: McCarthyism in Twentieth-Century America* (New York: Random House, 2001), xiv.
91 See "Lexington: Insurrection Revisionism," *The Economist* (July 31, 2021), 27.
92 Jonathan Rauch, *The Constitution of Knowledge: A Defense of Truth* (Washington, DC: Brookings Institution Press, 2021), 183.
93 See Richard Landes, "Millennialism," ed. James R. Lewis, *The Oxford Handbook of New Religious Movements* (Oxford: Oxford University Press, 2004), 351–2.
94 Butter, *The Nature of Conspiracy Theories*, 21.
95 Butter, *The Nature of Conspiracy Theories*, 119.

96 This issue is more fully developed in Chapter 4.
97 See Butter, *The Nature of Conspiracy Theories*, 150–63.
98 Wikipedia, "Conspiracy Theory," 1. (Accessed January 23, 2023).
99 See Lewis S. Feuer, *Ideology and the Ideologists* (Oxford: Oxford University Press, 1975).
100 Gregory Baum, *The Twentieth Century: A Theological Overview* (Maryknoll, NY: Orbis Books, 1999), 244.
101 See T.E. Clarke, "Fundamentalism and Prejudice," *The Way* (January, 1987), 33–41.
102 Reuel L. Howe, *The Miracle of Dialogue* (New York: Seabury Press, 1963), 37.
103 William Isaacs, *Dialogue: And the Art of Thinking Together* (New York: Doubleday, 1999), 87.
104 See Butter, *The Nature of Conspiracy Theory*, 140–2.
105 The lamentation psalms constitute a third of all the psalms. See Walter Brueggemann, *The Psalms and the Life of Faith* (Minneapolis: Fortress Press,1995), 33–111, 217–34, 258–82.
106 Bernard Haring, *Free and Faithful in Christ: Moral Theology for Priests and Laity Vol. 2* (Quezon City: Claretian Publications, 1985), 42.
107 Haring, *Free and Faithful in Christ*, 42. See Robert W. Wall, "The Acts of the Apostles," ed. Leander E. Keck, *The New Interpreter's Bible Vol. X* (Nashville: Abingdon, 2002), 98–9.
108 See John L. McKenzie, *The Dictionary of the Bible* (London: Geoffrey Chapman, 1965), 667.
109 See Arbuckle, *Culture, Inculturation, and Theologians* (Collegeville, MN: Liturgical Press, 2010), 169.
110 Justin the Martyr cited by Leonardo Boff, *Church, Charism and Power: Liberation Theology and the Institutional Church* (London: SCM Press, 1985), 94.
111 Thomas Aquinas, *De Veritate*, q. 1. A.8.
112 For a fuller description of this mystery, see Gerald A. Arbuckle, *Laughing With God: Humor, Culture, and Transformation* (Collegeville, MN: Liturgical Press, 2008), 111–13.
113 Karl Rahner, *Belief Today* (London: Sheed and Ward, 1973), 4.
114 John Paul II, Encyclical Letter *Fides et Ratio* (Faith and Reason 1998), (Vatican: Vatican Press, 1998), par. 71.
115 Barkun, *A Culture of Conspiracy*, 3.
116 Adolf Hitler stated in September 18, 1922: "We in Germany have come to this: that sixty-million people see its destiny lie at the will of a few dozen Jewish bankers. . . . No salvation is possible until the bearer of disunion, the Jew, has been rendered powerless to harm." See Adolf Hitler, *My New Order* (New York: Reynal and Hitchcock, 1941), 45.

3 Conspiracy Theorizing Drives Scapegoating, Populism and Polarization

> Conspiracy theories . . . function . . . as a basis for stigmatization.
> (Michael Barkun)[1]

> Scapegoating conspiracism responds to resentment and feelings of powerlessness by singling out a segment of the population as the cause of cruelly disappointed expectations.
> (Russell Muirhead and Nancy L. Rosenblum)[2]

> The virus of polarization and animosity permeates our way of thinking, feeling and acting.
> (Pope Francis)[3]

This chapter explains that:

- Scapegoating is an integral quality of conspiracy theories.
- Scapegoating is the blaming and marginalizing of innocent people for someone else's troubles.
- Cultural traumas intensify scapegoating.
- Both the Old Testament and the New Testament condemn scapegoating.

In the previous chapter the reality of scapegoating as an integral quality of conspiracy theorizing was lightly touched upon. The aim of this chapter is to go further, namely to focus on the nature, origin, and evil qualities of scapegoating; and to critique scapegoating according to Gospel values. Scapegoating formally transforms malevolent judgements of others from a world of shared secrets in gossip directly into the public arena. In scapegoating, an innocent person or a group is publicly charged for someone else's troubles; it is a way of deflecting blame and responsibility.

Conspiracy theorizing drives scapegoating. Recall the time when "the chief priests and the Pharisees called a meeting of the council" (John

DOI: 10.4324/9781003472162-4

11:47) because they feared the popularity of Jesus with the people following his raising to life of Lazarus. Caiphas, the high priest, listening to the gossip of the council, finally and publicly stated: "You know nothing at all! You do not understand that it is better for you to have one man die for the people than to have the whole nation destroyed" (John 11: 50). Later, rather than evaluating their own behaviour, the chief priests would reassure Pilate, "We have no king except Caesar" (John 19:16). They concocted that Jesus wanted to be king. Jealousy and self-preservation motivated the council's scapegoating of Jesus, which led to his public execution.

Defining Scapegoating[4]

Scapegoating, or witch-hunting as it is commonly termed, is the process of passionately searching for and eliminating agents, if possible, especially the relatively powerless, and those already disliked or stigmatized, who are believed to be causing harm to individuals and groups, for example, the poor and immigrants. By passing the blame for their afflictions on to others, people are able conveniently to distract themselves and others from the real causes and the efforts they must make to remove them. The power inequality between the genders and the active devaluation of females are among the fundamental causes of violence against inside or outside the home. If a man's position is threatened in the wider society, he can still create or keep power through threatening violence. The female partner (or powerless child) becomes the scapegoat for the man's feelings of fear and inadequacy.[5] Adolfo Hitler censured Jewish people for the global woes of the Great Depression;[6] Donald Trump falsely charged immigrants for introducing coronavirus into the United States;[7] and today in South Africa politicians are rivalling with each other to see who is able to blame immigrants most forcefully for the nation's self-inflicted economic troubles.[8]

The greater or more intense the economic, political, and cultural chaos and consequent fear of the unknown, the more frequent and persistent is the scapegoating. Conspiracy theories feed mass witch-hunting movements, moral panics, or crazes. Societies become polarized. Putting aside the rules of rationality, people inspired by charismatic leaders vengefully and simplistically name individuals or groups they claim are causing the chaos. The unscrupulous leaders may, for example, be witch-doctors in premodern societies or populist secular or religious leaders in our modern world.

Shame, envy, jealousy, and fear are among the formidable emotions behind scapegoating (see *Propositions 4* and *9*, Chapter 1). For example, one who is shamed, in order to flee an inner sense of inadequacy, turns in rage on a person or group that is envied and is blamed for their problems.[9] Tom Douglas speaks of "strategic scapegoating" in modern politics which, he says, may be shame-driven:

> The driving force behind a great deal of public scapegoating encased in conspiracy theories in modern times seems to be related to the possibility of exposure, a fear of being found out. . . . Hence the powerful need to dissemble, to deny with as much authority as possible, to deflect and so look for others to take the blame.[10]

Sometimes the term "stigmatization" is used as a substitute for the word "scapegoating," but there is a significant difference in meaning. Sociologically a "stigma" is a social quality that devalues an individual or a group. There are socially defined stigmas of the body, for example, deformities; of assumed character, such as being gay; having a criminal record; and of social collectivities, for example, youth, the poor, a religion, tribe, nation, immigrant, culture. The fact that people suffer stigmas does not mean that at this moment they are scapegoated. It means that, when the need arises, they are the ones most likely to be scapegoated by the dominant power group for problems for which they are not responsible.[11]

Origins of Scapegoating

> The logic of scapegoating . . . is based on animal narcissism and hidden fear.
> (Ernest Becker)[12]

Pope Francis writes with deep sadness about the current world scene:

> the temptation to build a culture of walls, to raise walls, walls of the heart, walls on the land, in order to prevent . . . encounter with other cultures, with other people . . . [The] outside world ceases to exist and leaves only "my" world, to the point that others . . . become only "them."[13]

There seems to be a basic need in all cultures for human beings to avoid responsibility and to transfer evil to others. The comic dramatist W.S. Gilbert has the Lord High Executioner in the opera *Mikado* sing:

> As some day it may happen that a victim must be found,
> I've got a little list-I've got a little list,
> Of society offenders who might well be underground,
> And who never would be missed-who never would be missed.

Through symbols, myths, and rituals, all cultures have an inbuilt tendency to create boundaries with potentially powerful feelings dividing "us" from "them," unless they proactively prevent this occurring. This is the social disease of ethnocentrism. The English poet Rudyard Kipling describes ethnocentrism in this way: "All nice people like Us are We, and everyone else is They."[14] The media can play a key role in developing the language of exclusion through their cutting back of complex realities to simplified popularizing binaries such as black/white, young/old, "which are then joined to estimations of moral worth such as degenerate/civilized . . . respectable/rough. This contributes to the creation of images of the 'other' as abnormal, distant, outside and not us."[15] Since the "other" is not like us they can be treated with disdain. Sociologist Jock Young describes this as a method of cultural essentialism that "allows people to believe in their inherent superiority while being able to demonise the other, as essentially wicked, stupid or criminal."[16]

A *moral* panic is a specific type of contemporary ethnocentrism. In a moral panic a particular individual or group of people is defined, especially through extensive mass media publicity, as a threat to the values and interests of the dominant society. A moral panic is an experience of widespread anxiety or hysteria; social deviates must be identified, bullied, and punished, and then moral values will once again be restored to society. "Evil ones" are stigmatized and socially excluded, so life can get back to "normal." Moral panics deflect attention away from more serious structural and social issues.[17] The word "panic" "implies not only fear but fear that is wildly exaggerated and wrongly directed."[18] President Donald Trump's border ban on Muslims and his vilification of illegal immigrants as rapists and murderers fostered a moral panic against specific groups of people, scapegoating them for "stealing our jobs."[19] In September 2001 the Australian government prevented, contrary to international law, 433 Afghanistan asylum seekers from landing in Australia after they had been rescued from drowning by a Norwegian freighter. Their decision had widespread local support. It was a good case of moral panic. The number of them trying to land was small but many Australians felt that the refugees, if they landed, would undermine the Anglo-Saxon cultural identity of the nation.[20]

Ethnocentrism: Theories of Origins

Now let us examine more deeply the origins of ethnocentrism. Three authors in particular, historian and philosopher Rene Girard, psychologist Isabel Menzies Lyth, and anthropologist Mary Douglas, further explain the polarizing origin and power of ethnocentrism and scapegoating.[21]

Violence Theory

Rene Girard (1923–2015) has published an extensive thesis on scapegoating.[22] In his theory of violence he distinguishes between "constructive" and "reciprocal" violence. The former, constructive violence, contributes to the cohesion of the group, and scapegoating is a significant way to achieve this. Reciprocal violence is violence directed by an individual against another, leading ultimately to the destruction of the group. The origins of reciprocal violence are to be found in the idea of a human self that is primarily imitative or mimetic. We come to be who we are by imitating other people. They become models for what we want to be, but a problem arises when these models become rivals and barriers to our development. They then are branded as enemies wanting to destroy us. When tensions reach an explosive level so that society's existence is threatened, then the scapegoating dynamic becomes operative.

Scapegoats are chosen and they exhaust the violence of the group, so peace is temporarily restored. Society is pure once more. The cycle is repeated whenever reciprocal violence is in danger of getting out of hand.[23] For Girard, the mimetic self and scapegoating together mould the dynamics of all religions, cultures, and societies. The scapegoat is sacrificed for the sake of community well-being. Through scapegoating the community protects itself from its own destructive violence, restores harmony, and reinforces social bonds.

Girard claims that, with the advent of the Judeo-Christian way of life, scapegoating is no longer so effective in guaranteeing social harmony. God reveals the divine opposition to scapegoating by coming out on the side of the victim and against constructive violence. Jesus Christ, as foretold by the prophets, ends the cycle of vengeance: Christ dies asking forgiveness for his executioners who do not understand what they are doing (Luke 23:34).[24] Scapegoating is a lie invented by society to achieve an illusory feeling of peace. This is the message of Christ's life, death, and resurrection. Christ's mission is "to bear witness to the truth" (John 18: 37) of the innocence of all victims of violence, and that violence in each individual and society can be controlled through God's love. Christians reject this message every time they fail to act according to the Gospel principles of nonviolence; for example, their persecution of Jews and heretics has helped to perpetuate scapegoating down through the centuries.[25]

Social scientists reviewing the links between sex and violence have also stressed the role of sacrificial displacement or scapegoating. Many consider that the power inequality between the genders and the active devaluation of females are among the fundamental causes of violence against women inside and outside the home.[26] If the man's position is threatened in the wider society, he can still create or keep power in the home through threatening violence. He can evoke the centuries' old conspiracy theory that women are inherently unable to think and behave intelligently. The female partner (or powerless child) becomes the scapegoat for the man's feeling of fear and inadequacy.[27]

Splitting Theory

Splitting is "a cultural and psychodynamic process whereby individuals and groups, in an effort to cope with the doubts, anxieties and conflicting feelings caused by difficult work, isolate different elements of experience, often to protect the perceived good from the bad."[28] This division then forms a social defence,[29] that is, a system of relationships that people feel protects them from cultural disintegration or loss of meaning.[30] People look for forms or frames to contain in their anxiety.[31] In *splitting* people seek unconsciously to contain their anxieties in dysfunctional ways by projecting their anxieties/fears on to an external individual or group.[32] The projecting group judges itself to be "good" and the victim of the projection is judged to be "bad." The "bad" is assumed to be the cause of all the fears and "evils" being experienced. That is, those who experience the "evils" are unable to cope with them themselves personally (or as groups), so they take the easier option of degrading whatever they see as unimportant. They "split off" what is negative in their experience and project it on to others. This results in a form of fundamentalism in which complex issues and problems are highly reduced to simplified problems or causes (e.g. "they are to blame for *all* my problems"). The feelings are so high that normally reasoned arguments that question the simplicity of the degrading process cannot be heard. The contemporary rise of extreme nationalism in Western democracies, with its anti-immigrant dynamic, is an example of splitting. In the midst of rapid social and economic changes people feel threatened; they want to feel good again, so the more immigrants are marked as "bad" or "useless for the economy," the more the locals feel good and in control of the threatening chaos.

Psychoanalyst Melanie Klien discovered that the unconscious dynamic of splitting begins very early in life; in early infancy, a child separates good and bad experiences of the same object (breast) or person (mother).[33] Klein points out that it is a sign of maturity for a person to accept the emotions of hate and love for the same person, without escaping into the false comfort of splitting as explained here.

The insight of splitting refines the anthropological explanation of scapegoating by introducing the notion of *projection*. When people feel threatened or inadequate, they can attribute these feelings and impulses to others as individuals or as groups. For example, when men cannot acknowledge their sense of vulnerability, they can imagine women are the vulnerable ones; poor whites refusing to admit their own feelings of inferiority may conclude that blacks are the inferior ones.

Pollution Theory and Tribalism

Muirhead and Rosenblum write that "[t]ribalism . . . fuels . . . conspiracism," and "tribalism is intimately related to scapegoating."[34] Mary Douglas' concept of social pollution helps to explain the connection between these realities. Social pollution does not refer to the intrinsic hygienic properties of things but rather to their symbolic qualities as "matter out of place."[35] For Douglas, when explaining her understanding of pollution, the object of our deepest anxieties is everyday dirt. It evokes an attitude, "ugh!," and demands a response, "clean-up!" What is considered dirty in some way or other pollutes or defiles what is clean and must be put aside. An appreciation of what causes things to be called dirty or clean, Douglas argues, may uncover the deepest mysteries of the moral order itself, the reasons that some societies renew and reaffirm their fundamental collective feelings and beliefs, while others do not even bother.[36]

The question is, why are some things branded dirty and other things clean? Why are shoes judged dirty when placed on the table, but clean when on the floor? It is the location that defines their dirtiness and its power to evoke a reaction. Ideas of dirt and feelings of being disgusted arise when things are outside their usual boundary system. Examples embrace how we consider our relation to hair, fingernails, and skin taken from the body, or pots and pans being placed in the bedroom away from the kitchen. As Douglas writes, "Dirt is the by-product of a systematic ordering and classification of matter, in so far as ordering involves rejecting inappropriate elements."[37] This means that what is thought to be dirty is relative. Douglas comments:

> It's a relative idea. Shoes are not dirty in themselves, but it is dirty to place them on the dining-table; . . . it is dirty to leave cooking utensils in the bedroom; . . . In short, our pollution behaviour is the reaction which condemns any object or idea to confuse or contradict cherished classifications.[38]

It is not just a question of factual location that condemns something as dirty or clean. Shoes are not dirty just because they are on the table rather than on the floor but because they *should* be on the floor, and *not* on the table. There is a moral quality to reality that renders the issue of classification, and misclassification, also as a matter of right and wrong. When we say that shoes should not be on the floor, we are not only stating a fact about "the mechanical appropriateness of nature, but a moral evaluation of that order."[39] Dread of pollution is like fear of immorality or sin.

Every human society and organization subscribe, mostly *unconsciously*, to rules of purity and pollution in some form or other. A culture is a purity system – that is, it tells people what is pure and clean, or evil, and therefore dangerous or polluting. The fear of pollution defines and protects the boundaries of a group. Pollution, as opposed to purity, interferes with the acceptable equilibrium, destroys or confuses desirable boundaries, and evokes destructive forces or conditions. As Douglas writes, "In short, our pollution behaviour is the reaction which condemns any object or idea likely to confuse or contradict cherished classifications."[40] Contemporary refugees trying to land in the United States, Australia, or Europe are daring to break orderly boundaries and thus are creating among citizens a fear of being "polluted." They are "them" and the self-righteous citizens are "we."[41] Caroline Elkins comments: "'Take Back Control' was Brexit's enduring slogan, a control that Britain ostensibly lost when it integrated with Europe and opened its doors to the continent's immigrants who further 'polluted' the nation."[42]

This pollution theory throws light on the power and rigidity of tribalism. The more tribal or closed-in cultures become, the more they fear the socially contaminating threats of other cultures. And the dominant driver of tribalism is always conspiracy theories.

The term "tribe" implies a large element of cultural solidarity and belonging based on strongly shared symbols myths, and rituals. Each tribal group takes the position of "thinking and feeling that anyone whose behaviour is not predictable or is peculiar in any way is slightly out of [their] mind, improperly brought up, irresponsible, psychopathic, politically motivated to a point beyond redemption, or just plain inferior."[43] Tribalism forbids members from connecting with people not of their tribes, and it also ostracizes members who dare to break the boundaries to connect with outsiders. Bitter and divisive tensions among tribes lead to polarization with less and less common ground fuelled by more and more outlandish conspiracy theories. Each tribe cultivates negative emotionally charged stereotypes and prejudices about its tribal neighbours, making dialogue across the boundaries difficult, if not impossible.[44]

Tribalism can rapidly morph into a greater and greater rigidity so that all hopes of sharing some common ground disappear. Reflecting on the contemporary American scene, Adrienne LaFrance writes:

> People build their political identities not around shared values but around hatred for their foes, a phenomenon known as "negative partnership". . . . The form of extremism we face is a new phase of domestic terror. . . . Unchecked, it promises an era of slow-motion anarchy. . . . As violence increases, so does distrust in institutions and leaders.[45]

Thus tribalism destroys democracies since politicians no longer have to concern themselves with ensuring that the community's real needs are satisfied but only that the "other side is faring worse."[46]

Tribal ethnocentrism reaches extremes when victims are dehumanized or declared to be racially inferior. Once people are declared non-human their tormenters have no restraints. Hence, Nazis stripped their victims of all protective dignity.[47] Hitler, inspired by his fundamentalist ideology, considered that particular peoples – Jews, people with disabilities, gays, and gypsies – endangered the purity of the Aryan race and had to be eliminated. In possibly the most horrible expression of this logic of pollution, he cleansed the fatherland by turning "dirty" Jews into "clean" soap.[48] Marine Le Pen, when heading a French populist political party, "insisted that Europe was being invaded by hordes of 'stinking' dark-skinned migrants and 'rat people' flowing in a 'river of sperm'"[49] Ukraine's government was falsely branded by Vladimir Putin as "openly neo-Nazi" and "pro-Nazi," controlled by "little Nazis."[50] Having branded the governed as inherently evil, Putin could legitimate the savagery of his troops in their invasion of Ukraine (see *Proposition 7*, Chapter 1).[51]

Cultural Trauma: Scapegoating and Polarization Intensify

As gossip flourishes in times of cultural disruption so also does scapegoating (see *Proposition 10*, Chapter 1). We fear the chaos of cultural disruption because culture responds to our need for normality, that is, consistency and felt order, the feeling of belonging. Nothing feels normal any more. Causes must be identified and blamed.[52] For example, the long and tragic history of witch-hunting attacks on Jews by Christians is well documented, beginning with the early Church.[53] Anti-Semitism is attitudes and actions against Jews based on the false belief that Jews are uniquely inferior, evil, and deserving of condemnation by their very nature or by historical dictates.[54] Jews were branded "as a league of sorcerers employed by Satan for the spiritual and physical ruination of Christendom,"[55] and this stereotyping justified their persecutory behaviour. The persecution of Jews erupted particularly whenever socioeconomic turmoil occurred and such was the case in the eleventh and twelfth centuries.

Cultural trauma, the severe form of cultural disruption, is the sudden, collective breakdown of order into chaos with disastrous consequences: "One can neither work nor play nor theorize with chaos. Chaos is pure terror. One must find forms and frames within which to contain it."[56] Scapegoating becomes extreme in cultural trauma.[57] Sociologist Neil Smelser defines cultural trauma as "an invasive and overwhelming event that is believed to undermine or overwhelm one or several ingredients of a culture or the culture as a whole." Cultural trauma occurs when "members of a collectivity feel they have been subjected to a horrendous event that leaves indelible marks upon their group consciousness, marking their memories forever, and changing their future identity in fundamental and irrevocable ways."[58] The founding mythology that emotionally and normatively binds the culture together giving people a sense of collective identity *ceases* to operate. With their culture shattered people lose their established sense of belonging. They feel stunned and mythologically rudderless, "subjected to a horrendous event that leaves indelible [paralysing] marks upon their group consciousness."[59]

Examples of cultural trauma abound in history such as the Great Depression, the Second World War, the depression that followed the global 2008 financial crash,[60] Covid-19. The 2008 financial disaster especially hit the poor hard: "The empirical findings . . . confirm the increasingly consistent story of 'two Americas' with the poor much less likely to be optimistic about their future than the rich."[61] But in the space of a few weeks Covid-19 beginning in 2020 further undermined social and economic order and predictability, again harshly impacting the poor and powerless, throwing entire nations into the awesome insecurities and numbness of chaos with long term human consequences.

In cultural trauma people are no longer able to find an adequate mythological response to the stresses they are undergoing. Rollo May is right: "The loneliness of mythlessness is the deepest and least assuageable of all. Unrelated to the past, unconnected with the future, we hang as if in mid-air."[62] The pandemic trauma left people and nations with the numbness of chaos, a collective evil, with enduring and indeterminate consequences. Existing polarizations intensified. Conspiracy theories abounded. Scapegoats must be found and blamed. When an event as massive and globally significant as the Covid-19 occurs, the political, social, and economic shocks take years and even generations to play out. They spin off in unpredictable directions. This quickly became startlingly evident as I now explain in more detail.

Pre-Covid-19

Before the pandemic, economic and social inequalities, the breeding ground of violence and racial tensions, both within and between nations, had been on the rise, exacerbated by the trauma of the 2008 financial crash.[63] Yascha Mounk cogently argued, in 2018, that three big happenings were driving the instability of liberal democracies.[64] *First* and most important, slow economic growth and the that gaps between the rich and poor were rapidly widening; people in industrial areas destroyed by economic failures become avid supporters of the enticing unreality of populist leaders such as Donald Trump and others.[65] *Second*, the recent surge in immigration in most important democracies was fuelling a backlash against ethnic and cultural pluralism; *third*, the expansion of social media was providing an opportunity for autocratic and fundamentalist voices to circumvent traditional media gatekeepers. The rise of digital technology "has favoured the spread of hate speech and conspiracy theory."[66] The Covid-19 pandemic significantly increased these realities. The consequences? The more unequal a society gets the more the political and social upheavals being driven by scapegoating conspiracy theories

Covid-19: Democracies Threatened

Democracy is experiencing its worst crisis since the tragic explosion of nationalism in the 1930s that ended with the Second World War. The cultural trauma born of Covid-19 has intensified political polarizations, nationalisms and severe economic depressions are socially and politically dangerous combinations.[67] The poverty of leadership, inequality, and economic stagnation have not helped. "In a world of increasing fundamentalist movements, of wall-builders, door-slammers, and drawbridge raisers,"[68] the dangers to world peace are again rapidly becoming evident. Pope Francis calls this a rebirth of nationalistic "narcissism . . . born of a certain insecurity and fear of the other that leads to rejection and the desire to erect walls for self-defence. . . . [The] sense of belonging to a single human family is fading."[69] Little wonder that there are a mass of different polarizing and scapegoating movements in the ascendancy offering simplistic solutions to political, economic and social problems. An ideal atmosphere for dangerous leaders to flourish.

Three contemporary polarizing global movements, fuelled by conspiracy theories, within and between nations stand out. Each claims to have the answer to the cultural traumas: fundamentalism, populism and autocracy. For analytical reasons I describe them separately but in reality they may share many qualities in common.

Rising Fundamentalism

The term 'fundamentalists' did not originally have a pejorative connotation, but this has radically changed. It now has a disparaging quality. It has been widely extended to define people who adhere to fundamentalism, that is, an historically recurring negative tendency particularly within Judeo-Christian-Muslim traditions, which occurs as an authoritarian religious reaction particularly to the fears of anomie or chaos evoked by postmodernism and contemporary crises.[70] The distinguishing aspects of fundamentalism are *nostalgia*, zeal to restore an unreal past, and its pervading religious element:

> [Fundamentalisms] are embattled forms of spirituality, which have emerged as a response to a perceived crisis. They are engaged in a

conflict with enemies whose secularist policies and beliefs seem inimical to religion itself.[71]

[Fundamentalism is] a specifiable pattern of religious militancy by which self-styled true believers attempt to arrest the erosion of religious identity, fortify the borders of the religious community, and create viable alternatives to secular structures and processes.[72]

James Hunter calls fundamentalism a form of "organized anger" and says that all fundamentalist groups "share the deep and worrisome sense that history has gone awry,"[73] the consequence of modernity and post-modernity. Perhaps a more relevant word than anger is 'rage.' Richard Antoun also emphasizes the emotional aspect of fundamentalism: it is "an orientation to the world, both cognitive and affective. The affective, or emotional, orientation indicates outrage and protest against (and also fear of) change and against a certain ideological orientation, the orientation of modernism."[74] Fundamentalists react to threats to their identity in aggressive ways, whether in the use of words and ideas or ballots or, in extreme incidents, bullets and bombs.

For most people fundamentalism in the modern world has become synonymous with a radical form of Islam. Islamic fundamentalism, such as the terrorist movements Hamas and Hezbollah,[75] has supplanted communism as the ghost haunting the Western consciousness – a ghost that looms ever larger following the deadly terrorist attacks on New York and Washington, DC, 11 September 2001,[76] and on Israel in 2023. Yet Islamic fundamentalist movements have received a disproportionate amount of media attention in recent times due to the physically violent nature of their actions.[77] This singling out of Islamic fundamentalists is unfortunate because fundamentalism in many shapes and forms is very much present in our Western societies though often less observably physically violent. Fundamentalist economic, political, nationalistic, religious movements are aplenty in the West. Right-wing, anti-immigrant movements are on the rise in Europe, United States, Australia and elsewhere. We in the West have to cease thinking of ourselves as "angelic and that Islam is the Devil incarnate."[78]

For example, in the late 1820s and 1830s the United States was in a period of cultural trauma. Older settlers resented the social and economic problems increasingly evident in the growing cities. Many feared for their jobs as the new immigrants, especially large numbers of Irish, were willing to work for minimal wages. Anti-Irish and consequently anti-Catholic bigotry intensified.[79] Protestant Americans were also suspicious about the institutional Catholic Church, believing it to be despotic, and holding values contrary to the American republic ideals.[80] Protestant leaders had become frightened by what they believed to be the dual dangers of Catholic growth and atheistic thinking. Not surprisingly anti-Catholic, pro-white fundamentalist political movements emerged, for example, the Know-Nothings in the South before the Civil War, the American Protective Association in the Mid-West at the end of the nineteenth century, and the Klu Klux Klan in the early twentieth century.[81] The Klan, a white supremacist sect, was founded as a terrorist movement, reaching its peak in the 1920s with over four million members. Their core belief is to restore America to being a white, Christian nation free from: drugs, homosexuality, immigration, and race-mixing which the Klan believed caused (and continues to cause) the nation's decline. Their terrorist activities led to numerous killings and hate crimes against their perceived enemies. In brief, the major issue in the mind of the Klan in the 1920s became "a struggle between 'the great mass of Americans of the old pioneer stock' and the 'intellectually mongrelized Liberals.'"[82] According to Hiram Wesley Evans (1881–1966), the Imperial Wizard of the Klan from 1922 to 1939, the Klan spoke for those struggling with the moral decay and economic distress of the twentieth century.

A later fundamentalist American example is the National Union for Social Justice was a fundamentalist reaction to the economic remedies of the New Deal. This extreme right-wing Union was led by a Catholic priest Father Charles Coughlin in a Michigan parish, a young pastor and skilled communicator. At first in his Sunday afternoon radio broadcasts he was a strong advocate of the New Deal: "Roosevelt or Ruin!" Supported by millions of supporters, he quickly and bitterly turned against Roosevelt, the slogan changing to: "Roosevelt *and* Ruin!" While asserting that the New Deal was communist inspired he adopted at the same time an overt anti-Semitism.[83]

Pope Francis identifies and critiques polarizing fundamentalist movements also in the contemporary Catholic Church:

> Fundamentalism is a sickness that is in all religions . . . Religious fundamentalism is not religious, because it lacks God. It is idolatry, like idolatry of money . . . We Catholics have some – and not some, many – who believe in the absolute truth and go ahead dirtying the other with calumny, with disinformation, and doing evil.[84]

Populism

The term *populism* is applied to a variety of contemporary political crusades and is defined as: "a thin-centered ideology that considers society is ultimately separated into two homogenous and antagonistic camps, 'the pure people' versus 'the correct elite', and which argues that politics should be an expression of the *volonte generale* (general will) of the people."[85] Populism polarizes groups into the left and right, thus greatly weakening the political middle ground. Populists on the right denigrate liberal structures "such as science and rule of law as facades for a plot by the deep state against the people. They subordinate facts and reason to tribal emotion."[86] Those on the left assert, for example, that "the marketplace of ideas is rigged just for the others. What masquerades as evidence and argument, they say, is really yet another assertion of raw power by the elite."[87]

Jonathan Rauch in his book, *The Constitution of Knowledge*, skilfully shows how trolling from the right and cancel culture on the left is making dialogue for truth difficult, if not impossible, in populist times.[88] The term 'cancel culture' is a severe act of public shaming, shunning, boycotting, an unqualified rejection of whatever the opposition says or approves. Adversaries are scapegoated as morally contemptible, totally unworthy of dialogue. Democracies cannot long survive when masses of people are condemned outright as disgusting and contemptible.[89]

Populist Leaders

Populist leaders with the use of grievance-fuelled language and behaviour assert that innocent citizens are "beset by remote, powerful and malign enemies."[90] The elites, who must be named and marginalized or silenced, are described as unlawfully trampling upon the rights, values, and voice of the legitimate people.[91] By scapegoating an entire elite as corrupt and the democratic system as manipulated "against the common man, the populists" are helping "to create a demand for an outsider – a strongman who would take on the crooked globalist elites and stand up for the ordinary man."[92] British author David Goodhart comments: "Populists . . . tend not to be interested in the complexities of policy and . . . usually offer merely simple solutions to complex problems. The problem with simple solutions [of populist leaders] is that they raise expectations that are almost always disappointing, which then encourages even simpler or more radical solutions in a downward spiral of anger and denunciation."[93] Authoritarian populists, well aided by spin doctors, skilfully "manipulate information to boost their popularity with the public." They then "use that popularity to consolidate political control, all the while pretending to be democratic, avoiding or at least camouflaging violent repression."[94]

Populist leaders have this in common: they feed on the cultural trauma that people feel is overwhelming them; supported by conspiracy theories they promise simple solutions to complex problems and nefarious forces must be scapegoated and destroyed, even if this means breaking laws and traditions; they surround themselves with sycophantic staff who must never challenge the leader's behaviour. Like fake news, claims of misinformation or disinformation have become a default position for populists who do not like to listen to a dissenting opinion or to get in their way.

Too often populist leaders are out for personal power, not the welfare of deeply grieved people. American writer Mark Danner comments on Donald Trump: "By virtue of Trump's embodied grievance, his shamelessness, and his daring and skill at shaping a narrative – and then, when it is debunked, shaping another – Trump proves himself victorious, again and again, in attracting and holding eyeballs, which are the golden currency of our age."[95]

Populist leaders are narcissistic people. Narcissists are focused only on themselves as individuals; narcissism is self-admiration taken to an extreme. In consequence, narcissists

> lack emotionally warm, caring, and loving relationships with other people . . . [and they] manipulate and cheat to get ahead, surround themselves with people who look up to them . . . exploiting people and viewing others as tools to make themselves look and feel good.[96]

Commitments of all kinds are highly fragile, for every relationship, even marriage, is dispensable if it fails to serve the self-fulfilment aspirations of the narcissist.[97]

To summarize. Populist leaders exemplify these qualities with varying degrees of intensity. They:

- Pronounce naïve solutions to multifaceted problems in chaotic times.
- Ignore acceptable research that questions or contradicts these solutions.
- Personalize leadership by fostering a narcissistic personality cult.
- Bypass normal structures of government, thus creating more and more unmanageable chaos.
- Manipulate mass media to conceal truths.
- And/or their followers invent supportive conspiracy theories.
- Protect themselves from opposition by appointing sycophants.
- Refuse to be accountable for their actions.
- Scapegoat people when their simplistic solutions fail.

Authoritarian populist leaders are now moulding the direction of world politics.[98] They reject democracy, as Erdogan said: "Democracy is like a tram that you ride, until you get to your destination."[99] In Europe we have: Marine Le Pen, leader of the Front National in France, once compared Muslims praying in the French street to the Nazi Occupation; Geert Wilders, Party for Freedom, believes that Muslim immigration should be halted; Siv Jensen, leader of the Progress Party in Norway, achieved large popular gains through her attacks on Muslim immigration; in Hungary, Viktor Orban ratcheted up his anti-immigrant, anti-Muslim rhetoric; in Germany, in early 2016, the Alternative for Germany Party (AFD), achieved double-digit results in elections in three German states and the party officials have said it may be necessary to shoot at migrants trying to enter the country illegally and they have mooted the idea of banning mosques;[100] anti-democratic Jair Bolsonaro, former Brazilian president; and Giorgia Meloni's populist party in Italy, the Brothers of Italy.

In the United States when populist Trump first began to campaign for presidency with the catchcry "Make America Great Again," the nation was significantly divided. For liberals, the chief concern for the past thirty-five years is the unfairness of the economy – virtual wage stagnation for most workers, huge gains for the top 1 per cent, and the lax regulatory and enforcement regimes that have permitted these outcomes, along with slow recovery from the 2008 recession. For conservatives, for about the same period, the main worry is what is broadly called "culture," by which is really meant the anger and resentment felt by older white Americans about the fact that the country is no longer "theirs" and that their former status and authority no longer seem what they once were.[101] He expressed hatred of the "other" by describing illegal immigrants as rapists and murderers; claiming that the Mexicans and Chinese and others had stolen their jobs; and insisting that allies in Europe and Asia were calculating freeloaders usurping the protections of American power. This is the populist creating fear in order to legitimize the politics of exclusion.[102] His technique was to warn Americans that they are the victims of financial and political conspiracies that he would quickly break apart. His ability to target his supporters' anger and insecurities became unrivalled in American politics. He became "the grand master of grievance."[103] The more vulgar and prejudiced he became, the more his extensive following increased. In this, he is

> taping into a political tradition with deep roots. . . . The "American First" movement of the early 1940s accused decadent Europeans and well connected Jews of conspiring to drag America into a new world war. In the 1960s the John Birch Society saw communist cunning at every turn.[104]

Trump was elected as president in 2016 despite his well-publicized "narcissism and cheerleading for torture . . . racism, misogyny, and xenophobia."[105] He "stoked fears, incited hatreds, and sown doubts about American leadership in the world, and about the future of democracy itself."[106] The fears proved right. He spent four years intensifying this national division with global consequences. As a populist,[107] Trump became a "rage machine"[108] striking out at whatever his followers felt angry and offended about even if this meant scores of false statements, boasting, and scapegoating. In brief, once in power Trump immediately demonized his predecessor and began to destroy as much of the previous administration as possible, such as Obamacare, international trade agreements, and immigration policies. He exemplified many of the nastiest qualities of a scapegoating and narcissistic populist leader, for example: making himself the centre of a personality cult, cultivating a personality conceptualizing "the value of truth only in terms of whether it is convenient to him,"[109] giving simplistic solutions to complex issues and in the process claiming his opponents are dangerous and corrupt elites, "immoral . . . illegitimate, unfit, contemptible, un-American or . . . 'disgusting'."[110]

Many of Trump's followers colluded in this dehumanizing rhetoric. For four years, by his constant attack on presidential norms and conventions of government, including his refusal to accept the legitimacy of the election process and provoking the mob assault on the Capitol, Trump helped to undermine trust which is the foundation of democracy. By Trump's failure to condemn outright the white nationalists actively expressing their hate in Charlottesville in August 2017, he seemed to confirm his xenophobic preferences. He brought white nationalists and fascist sympathizers "into mainstream politics for the first time in living memory."[111] Thus Trump revived the residual myth that the following quotation from historian Robert Parkinson describes, namely, that African Americans and Native Americans were excluded from the nation's founding history – a myth of fundamentalism that still haunts the present:

> "Good" blacks and Indians were all but invisible in patriot newspapers throughout the conflict (Revolution of Independence). Rather they were lumped together, as Jefferson would in the Declaration, as "domestic insurrectionists" and "merciless savages." The totality of these printed stories created a convincing interpretation; . . . they were not eligible for any of the benefits of American independence.[112]

Boris Johnson,[113] a populist leader with demagogic tendencies and abetted by conspiracy theories, was elected Britain's prime minister in 2019.[114] His inept populist qualities quickly became evident when Covid-19 hit Britain.[115] He was slow to take the pandemic seriously despite the fact that countries in Europe, such as Italy, Denmark, Spain, and France, had gone into full lockdown. Moreover, when finally the country did impose restrictions – light at first – it was ill-prepared to undertake key precautions such as testing for the virus, identifying a contact-app, stop visits to aged-care homes. Vague announcements came from government, at times minimizing the risks of the virus and failing to report the seriousness of the rising death toll. Even when the second wave of the virus hit Britain, the government kept publishing a series of ever-changing orders which were broken with impunity by their own officials.[116]

Between March 2 and June 12, 2020, it is estimated that nearly 20,000 residents in care homes in England and Wales died due to Covid-19.[117]

Autocracy

Autocracy is on the rise in parts of the world, that is, government by one person or a small group with unlimited power. Existing democracies are threatened by internal and external forces.[118] While the world's attention was on the Covid-19 pandemic, autocrats took advantage to grab more power.[119] Dictatorial governments in the Philippines, China, Russia, Turkey, Bulgaria, El Salvador, and Brazil have all assumed emergency powers; Bulgaria has used the virus as an excuse to repress the Roma minority.[120] Dictators may pretend to be democrats. They may hold multiparty elections and even claim to have won 90 per cent of the vote but behind the façade of competence and honesty is brutality.[121] In August 2020, peaceful protests in Belarus against elections rigged by President Alexander Lukashenko were met by ruthless repression.[122] In the Balkans, where political trust is low, many people believed that their governments were lying about there even being a virus; in Bosnia prominent people were promoting conspiracy theories in order to conceal the realities of the Covid-19 virus infections.[123] Vladimir Putin, in his nationwide address, on February 21, 2023, re-affirmed his conspiracy theory that "We were doing everything possible to solve this problem peacefully [in Ukraine but] it is them who are culpable for the war."[124]

In the United States "the Trump administration fully earned its reputation for authoritarianism, demagogy, and anti-pluralism."[125] Trump's attitudes have not changed. When speaking at a Veterans Day, 2023, occasion, he vilified in distinctly anti-democratic language his domestic adversaries and critics as "vermin" who will "do anything . . . to destroy America and to destroy the American dream."[126] This led Tom Nichols of *The Atlantic* to write: "The former president, after years of espousing authoritarian beliefs, has fully embraced the language of fascism."[127] "Donald Trump's very candidacy," writes Zanner Minton Beddoes, "undermines American democracy. That the Republican Party would nominate a man who tried to overturn the results of the previous presidential election dims America as a democratic beacon."[128] On October 25, 2023, Republicans unanimously voted for Mike Johnson to lead the House of Representatives. *The Economist* reported that he "has indulged some of his party's worst impulses in recent years. He voted against certifying the 2020 election results and lobbied House Republicans to support a long-shot lawsuit to invalidate electoral-college votes in several states won by Joe Biden."[129] Only time will tell whether or not the American Constitution is strong enough to prevent autocracy taking a firm root in the country. Certainly "something 'morbid' seems to be happening in present-day America."[130]

Scriptural Critique

Both Testaments condemn scapegoating. For example, in the Old Testament three vulnerable groups of people are often singled out for special concern: widows, orphans, and strangers. In the Book of Exodus the Israelites are left in no doubt what they must do:

> You must not molest or oppress aliens, for you yourselves were once aliens in Egypt. You will not ill-treat widows or orphans; if you ill-treat them in any way . . . I shall certainly hear their appeal, my anger will be roused and I shall put you to the sword; then your own wives will be widows and your children orphans.
>
> (Exod 22:20-23)

God reminds the Israelites that they were once vulnerable aliens in Egypt until God rescued them from their slavery: "You must not infringe the rights of the foreigner or the orphan . . . Remember that you were once a slave in Egypt and that Yahweh your God redeemed you from that" (Exod 24:17-18).[131]

The Good Samaritan Parable

The Gospel is about love and justice. Scapegoating and suchlike behaviour are condemned as evil: "And you were once estranged and hostile in mind, doing evil deeds, he has now reconciled in his fleshly body through death, so as to present you holy and blameless and irreproachable before him" (Col 1:21-22). In the Good Samaritan parable[132] Samaritans are branded as religiously, culturally, and racially inferior by the more powerful Jews (Luke 10:25-37). But, Jesus in the person of the main actor, the Good Samaritan, condemns such behaviour. The Samaritan despised by the Jews goes immediately to aid of the gravely injured Jew.

The philosopher Charles Taylor, when writing on the foundations of Western civilization, concludes that this story of the Good Samaritan "can be seen as one of the original building blocks out of which our modern universalist moral consciousness has been built."[133] Social ethicist Chris Marshall writes that the parable "carries tremendous rhetorical power, for it evokes one of the most seminal narratives in the Western cultural tradition." He further writes: "Indeed, it is hard to think of another story that has been more influential in moulding personal and political virtue. . . . It is a story that still serve, even in contemporary secular society, as a useful reference point for measuring policy options."[134] A sign of the story's remarkable legacy is simply the continuing widespread use in society of the phrase "good Samaritan" as an example of selfless concern to come to the aid of others in need.[135] Martin Luther King, Jr., insisted that the parable's mandate is not just about charity but charity accompanied by political, structural, and systemic conversion founded on justice.[136]

There are five foundational truths contained in the story. The first truth is: *Creation is a Gift of God*. All life must be respected as coming from God. Human persons mirror God's power, in the sense that they think and act freely, but this freedom must be exercised in ways that respect the purpose of the Creator. Respect for human dignity is a value from which other values flow. Racism is an evil, a denial of God's gift of creation; poverty is the deprivation of the social structures and personal opportunities to live out God's plan and is an evil. Hospitality is another value that flows from this truth. When we are hospitable to a stranger, we are only sharing what ultimately belongs to God. Above all, however, the Samaritan is motivated by the love of God and neighbour.

The second truth is: *Commitment to Stewardship*. We are called to co-create with God: that is, to continue God's creation in the world in ways that mirror the dignity of God. This truth contains the core values of justice, mercy, compassion, and empathy. Because all creation comes from God, we must use it as stewards of God. Compassion has an interesting origin. "The Samaritan traveller . . . was moved with compassion" (Luke 10:33). Compassion is a value originally founded on kinship obligations, whether natural or symbolic.[137] The Hebrew word is derived from the word for *womb*, implying the need of one person to sympathize for another because they are born of the same mother. God is that mother, and we are all children of that womb and must accordingly feel with, and care for, each other as brothers and sisters. Thus the Samaritan feels the inner pain of marginalization that the victim – his brother – is experiencing.

The third truth is: *Commitment to Solidarity*. There is no support for individualism in the parable. In the Jewish tradition, people are expected to work together for the good of all in imitation of God's desire to build community with the Israelites: "I shall fix my home among you. . . . I shall be among you; I shall be your God and you will be my people" (Lev 26:11-12). The values of solidarity, unity, collaboration, dialogue, and mutuality are marks of an authentic community. The victim's pain of marginalization reminds the Samaritan of his own similar experience and his need for community.[138] Marcus Mescher writes: "Solidarity is equality and mutuality expressed in an inclusive community of belonging in partnership for just social, economic and political structures."[139] He cites ethicist David Hollenbach: "Solidarity is not only a virtue to be enacted by persons one at a time. It must be expressed in the economic, cultural, political, and religious institutions that shape society. Solidarity is a virtue of communities as well as individuals."[140]

The fourth truth is: *Commitment to Help People Who Are the Poor*. In the Scriptures, the phrases "people who are poor" and "the little ones" commonly refer to those who, through no fault of their own, are powerless in society. Structures of oppression such as institutional racism condemn them to economic, social, and political poverty. In the parable, Jesus identifies with the actions of the Samaritan. His primary concern in his ministry is to be with those who are marginalized in society. By his actions and words, Jesus frequently repeats this message: "I was hungry and you gave me food. . . . I was a stranger and you made me welcome" (Matt 25:35). Jesus becomes so closely identified with people who are poor that, when we refuse them justice, we are refusing him (Matt 25:31-46).

The fifth truth is: *Commitment to a Prophetic Role*. In the parable, to be a prophet is to remind people of the foundational truths when they ignore them: "The task of prophetic imagination is to cut through the numbness, to penetrate the self-deception."[141] But be prepared to take the consequences of doing so. On the bandit-infested road, the Samaritan not only risks his life for the victim but also, because of his actions, suffers further marginalization from both the Hebrew people and those of his own culture. Christ, the ultimate Good Samaritan, will, of course, give his life in the service of others no matter the cost.

In brief, the potential for gossip, conspiracy theorizing, and scapegoating is within every human heart.[142] As explained, these behaviours are often closely linked with feelings of fear, uncertainty, or being out of control, and it is common that personal and/or cultural crises encourage such reactions in people. Scapegoating falsely focuses on an external cause of problems thus negating or lessening the guilt of the agent; it also makes people feel bonded as they unite with others to scapegoat the victims. Yet the commandment "Neither shall you bear false witness against your neighbor" (Deut 5:20) applies to all forms of scapegoating. Just as Adam, in the Genesis myth, tries to blame Eve for what has happened rather than admit his own role in the incident, every person has the capacity to blame others for their afflictions and to ignore their own role in causing them. Jesus condemns this process of shifting the blame on to others: "You hypocrite, first take the log out of your own eye, and then you will see clearly to take the speck out of your neighbor's eye" (Matt 7: 5). Gossip and scapegoating ultimately killed Jesus.

Summary Points

- Scapegoating (or witch-hunting), an integral quality of conspiracy theorizing, is a process of passing the blame for afflictions on to others (who are commonly innocent), thus distracting the real causes and the efforts to remove them.
- Ethnocentrism is at the root cause of scapegoating. It is the making of judgements about others by applying a group's own standards, regarding one's own culture as superior, and therefore mistrusting people from other cultures. Tribal ethnocentrism reaches extremes when victims are dehumanized or declared to be racially inferior. Once people are declared non-human their tormenters have no restraints.
- Populism feeds on corruption and unaddressed grievance. Populists dominate the media and foster social and political divisions by embodying grievance and shaping or supporting existing conspiracy theories. When a conspiracy theory is debunked they formulate another one. For example, Donald Trump as president exploited existing polarizing divisions of class, race, gender, and religion to achieve political power.[143]
- Autocracy is on the rise in parts of the world. Democracy is experiencing its worst crisis since the tragic explosion of nationalism in the 1930s and the dangers are rapidly becoming evident. Globally, democracy and human rights are in retreat; the number of democracies has been lessening.[144] Fragile democracies particularly are under threat in Africa and South America.
- Conspiracy-fed nationalisms and cultural/economic traumas are socially dangerous mixes; even "Western societies are currently regressing toward the authoritarian politics that is linked historically with economic insecurity."[145]
- The Good Samaritan parable highlights the universal truths and values of solidarity, compassion, and justice that must infuse all decision-making and behaviour.

Discussion Questions

1 Do the cultures you belong to, for example work, recreational, national, encourage you to look down on other peoples, even to blame them incorrectly for problems? Think of examples when Jesus condemned this behaviour.
2 Read 1 Corinthians 13:1–13. Here St. Paul says the more we love God the less the evils of narcissism, jealousy and envy will affect us. Why do you think this is so? Have you praised individuals or groups recently for something good they have done?

Notes

1 Michael Barkun, *A Culture of Conspiracy: Apocalyptic Visions in Contemporary America* (Berkeley, CA: University of California Press, 2013), 27.
2 Russell Muirhead and Nancy L. Rosenblum, *A Lot of People Are Saying: The New Conspiracism and the Assault on Democracy* (Princeton: Princeton University Press, 2019), 56.
3 "Pope Francis Decries 'Virus of Polarization' in the World," www.wsj.com/articles/pope-francis-decries-polarization-in-the-world-1479579352 (Accessed December 12, 2016).
4 "The origin of the term *scapegoat* is biblical – in a Mosaic ritual, one goat is chosen to be the symbolic carrier of the sins of the people. Although scapegoating today is secular not religious, it bears the ancient traces of moral fervor and sanctimony." Muirhead and Rosenblum, *A Lot of People are Saying*, 56.
5 See Helen L. Conway, *Domestic Violence and the Church* (Carlisle: Paternoster Press, 1998), 76–7.
6 See Gerald A. Arbuckle, *The Pandemic and the People of God: Cultural Impacts and Pastoral Responses* (Maryknoll, NY: Orbis Books, 2021), 48–9; and George M. Fredrickson, *Racism* (Melbourne: Scribe, 2002), 106.
7 See Cynthia Miller-Idriss, *Hate in the Homeland: The New Global Right* (Princeton, NJ: Princeton University Press, 56, 59–60.
8 See "Xenophobia in South Africa: Scapegoating Africans," *The Economist* (June 11, 2022), 11.
9 See Stephen Pattison, *Shame: Theory, Therapy, Theology* (Cambridge: Cambridge University Press, 2000), 116, 127.
10 Tom Douglas, *Scapegoats* (London: Routledge, 1995), 76–7.
11 See Erving Goffman, *Stigma: Notes on the Management of Spoiled Identity* (Englewood Cliffs: Prentice-Hall, 1964).
12 Ernest Becker, *Escape From Evil* (New York: Free Press, 1976), 109.
13 Pope Francis, Encyclical Letter *Fratelli Tutti* (On Fraternity of Social Friendships) (October 3, 2020), par.27.
14 Rudyard Kipling, *Debts and Credits* (London: Macmillan, 1926), 327–8.
15 Daphne Habibis and Maggie Walter, *Social Inequality in Australia: Discourses, Realities and Futures* (South Melbourne: Oxford University Press, 2015), 125.
16 Jock Young, *The Exclusive Society* (London: Sage, 1999), 109.
17 See Arbuckle, *Violence, Society, and the Church: A Cultural Approach* (Collegeville, MN: Liturgical Press, 2004), 141–4; Stanley Cohen, *Folk Devils and Moral Panics: The Creation of Mods and Rockers* (Oxford: Martin Robertson, 1980); Erich Goode and Nachman Ben-Yehuda, *Moral Panics: The Social Control of Deviance* (Oxford: Blackwell, 1994).
18 Philip Jenkins, *Moral Panic: Changing Concepts of the Child Molester in Modern America* (New Haven: Yale University Press, 1998), 6–7.

19 See Arbuckle, *Loneliness: Insights for Healing in a Fragmented World* (Collegeville, MN: Liturgical Press, 2018), 75.
20 See James Jupp, *From White Australia to Woomera: The Story of Australian Immigration* (Cambridge: Cambridge University Press, 2002), 193–9.
21 See Mary Douglas, *Purity and Danger: An Analysis of the Concepts of Pollution and Taboo* (London: Routledge and Kegan Paul, 1966).
22 See Arbuckle, *Violence, Society*, 138–9.
23 See Rene Girard, *Violence and the Sacred* (Baltimore: Johns Hopkins University Press, 1992), 4.
24 See Rene Girard, *Things Hidden Since the Foundation of the World* (Stanford: Stanford University Press, 1987), 219.
25 See Robert G. Hamerton-Kelly, *Sacred Violence: Paul's Hermeneutic of the Cross* (Minneapolis: Fortress Press, 1992), 12–39.
26 See David A. Wolfe and others, "Interrupting the Cycle of Violence," ed. David Wolfe and others, *Child Abuse* (Thousand Oaks: Sage, 1997), 106.
27 See Helen L. Conway, *Domestic Violence and the Church* (Carlisle: Paternoster Press, 1998), 76–7.
28 Gareth Morgan, *Images of Organization* (Beverly Hills: Sage Publications, 1986), 206.
29 The term "social defense" was first used by Isabel Menzies Lyth in 1961. See her paper "The Functioning of Social Systems as a Defense against Anxiety," *Human Relations*, no. 13 (1961).
30 See Larry Hirschhorn and Donald R. Young, "Dealing With Anxiety of Working Social Defenses as Coping strategy," eds. Manfred F.R. Kets de Vries and others, *Organizations on the Couch* (San Francisco: Jossey-Bass, 1991), 223.
31 See C. Fred Alford, "The Group as a Whole or Acting Out the Missing Leader," *International Journal of Group Psychotherapy*, vol. 45, no. 1 (1995): 133.
32 For fuller explanation see Isabel Menzies Lyth, "A Case Study in the Functioning of Social Systems as a Defense against Anxiety: A Report on a Study of the Nursing Service of a General Hospital," *Human Relations*, vol. 13 (1960): 95–121.
33 See Melanie Klein, *New Directions in Psychoanalysis* (London: Tavistock, 1955).
34 Muirhead and Rosenblum, *A Lot of People Are Saying*, 56.
35 Mary Douglas, *Purity and Danger: An Analysis of the Concepts of Pollution and Taboo* (London: Routledge and Kegan Paul, 1966), 36.
36 See Robert Wuthnow, James D. Hunter, Albert Bergesen and Edith Kurzweil, *Cultural Analysis* (London: Routledge and Kegan Paul, 1984), 85.
37 Douglas, *Purity and Danger*, 48.
38 Douglas, *Purity and Danger*, 48.
39 Wuthnow and Others, *Cultural Analysis*, 87.
40 Douglas, *Purity and Danger*, 36.

41 See Richard Alba and Nancy Foner, *Strangers No More: Immigration and the Challenges of Integration in North America and Western Europe* (Princeton: Princeton University Press, 2015), 2–16.
42 Caroline Elkins, *Legacy of Violence: A History of the British Empire* (London: The Bodley Head, 2022), 679.
43 Edward Hall, *Beyond Culture* (Garden City, NY: Anchor Press/Doubleday, 1977), 43.
44 See Susan Neiman, *Left Is Not Woke* (Cambridge: Polity Press, 2023), 11–56.
45 Adrienne LaFrance, "The New Anarchy," *The Atlantic* (April, 2023), 24, 25, 36. "A 2022 UC poll found that one in five Americans believes political violence would be 'at least sometimes' justified, and one in 10 believes it should be justified if it meant returning Trump to the presidency." Idem, 24.
46 Fintan O'Toole, "Defying Tribalism," *The New York Review of Books* (November 2, 2023), 18.
47 See Jonathan Glover, *Humanity: A Moral History of the Twentieth Century* (London: Jonathan Cape, 1999), 338–9.
48 See Alan Dundes, "A Study of German National Character Through Folklore," *Journal of Psychoanalytic Anthropology*, no. 4 (1981): 265–364.
49 Erirkur Bergmann, *Conspiracy and Populism*, 173.
50 Anton Troianovski, "Why Vladimir Putin Invokes Nazis to Justify His Invasion of Ukraine," *The New York Times* (March 17, 2022) (PDF).
51 See Philip Short, *Putin: His Life and Times* (London: The Bodley Head, 2022), 661–2.
52 See Arbuckle, *Violence, Society*, 144–50.
53 See Luke T. Johnson, "The New Testament Anti-Jewish Slander and the Conventions of Ancient Polemic," *Journal of Biblical Literature*, vol. 108, no. 3 (1989): 419–41; George M. Smiga, *Pain and Polemic: Anti-Judaism in the Gospels* (New York: Paulist Press, 1992); Mike Rothschild, *Jewish Space Lasers: The Rothschilds and 200 Years of Conspiracy Theories* (Hoboken, NJ: Melville House, 2023).
54 See Paul E. Grosser and Edwin G. Halperin, *The Causes and Effects of Anti-Semitism* (New York: Philosophical Library, 1978), 5.
55 Norman Cohn, *Warrant for Genocide* (Harmondsworth: Penguin, 1970), 12.
56 C. Fred Alfond, "The Group as a Whole or Acting Out the Missing Leader," *International Journal of Group Psychotherapy*, vol. 45, no. 1 (1995): 133.
57 See Arbuckle, *The Pandemic and the People of God*, 39–62.
58 Jeffrey Alexander, quoted by Neil J. Smelser, "September 11, 2001, as Cultural Trauma," eds. Jeffrey C. Alexander, Ron Eyerman, Bernhard Gleeson, Neil J. Smelser, and Plotr Sztompka, *Cultural Trauma and Collective Identity* (Berkeley: University of California Press, 2004), 265.

59 Jeffrey C. Alexander, "Toward a Theory of Cultural Trauma," in ibid., 1.
60 The crash evoked an array of anti-European Union movements and anti-globalization nationalists. In France and the United Kingdom, fundamentalist slogans became popular like "France for the French" and "England for the English." See George Makari, *Of Fear and Strangers: A History of Xenophobia* (New Haven: Yale University Press, 2021), 246–65.
61 Carol Graham, *Happiness for All? Unequal Hopes and Lives in Pursuit of the American Dream* (Princeton, NJ: Princeton University Press, 2017), 118.
62 Rollo Mary, *The Cry for Myth* (New York: Delta, 1991), 99. Italics in original.
63 See Arbuckle, *The Pandemic*, xiii–xix; Martin Sandbu, *The Economics of Belonging* (Princeton: Princeton University Press, 2020), 17–18, 28–9, 56–62; Robert D. Putnam and Shaylyn Romney Garrett, *The Upswing: How America Came Together a Century Ago and How We Can Do It Again* (New York: Simon and Schuster, 2020), 186–99; Martin Wolf, *The Crisis of Democratic Capitalism* (New York: Penguin Press, 2023), 83–117.
64 See Yascha Mounk, *The People Vs. Democracy: Why Our Freedom Is in Danger and How to Save It* (Cambridge, MA: Harvard University Press, 2018).
65 See Martin Sandbu, *The Economics of Belonging* (Princeton: Princeton University Press, 2020), 17–36, 192; Harriet Bradley, *Fractured Identities: Changing Patterns of Inequality* (Cambridge: Polity, 2016), 260–78; Simon Winlow, Steve Hall, and James Treadwell, *The Rise of the Right: English Nationalism and the Transformation of Working-Class Politics* (Bristol: Policy Press, 2017), 197–208.
66 Mounk, *The People Vs. Democracy*, 237; see Cynthia Miller-Idriss, *Hate in the Homeland: The New Global Far Right* (Princeton: Princeton University Press, 2020), 7–8, 20–2, 56–62. She emphasizes the disturbing fact of "mainstreaming extremism," that is, the spread of hateful and violent attitudes so that ever-more people share and promote them.
67 See Pippa Norris and Ronald Inglehart, *Cultural Backlash: Trump, Brexit and Authoritarian Populism* (Cambridge: Cambridge University Press, 2019), 464.
68 Madelaine Drohan, "Liberty Moves North," *The Economist* (October 29, 2016), 8.
69 Pope Francis, Encyclical Letter, *Fratelli Tutti* (On the Fraternity and Social Friendship) (Vatican, October 3, 2020), pars. 146, 30.
70 See Gerald A. Arbuckle, *Fundamentalism at Home and Abroad: Analysis and Pastoral Responses* (Collegeville, MN: Liturgical Press, 2017), 1–29.
71 Karen Armstrong, *The Battle for God: Fundamentalism in Judaism, Christianity and Islam* (London: HarperCollins, 2001), xi.

72 R. Scott Appleby, *The Ambivalence of the Sacred: Religion, Violence, and Reconciliation* (Oxford: Rowman and Littlefield, 2000), 86.
73 James Hunter, cited in ed. Norman J. Cohen, *The Fundamentalist Phenomenon* (Grand Rapids: W. B. Eerdmans, 1990), 46.
74 Richard T. Antoun, *Understanding Fundamentalism: Christian, Islamic, and Jewish Movements* (Walnut Creek, CA: AltaMira Press, 2001), 3.
75 Arbuckle, *Fundamentalism*, 133–58.
76 See Stuart Sim, *Fundamentalist World: The New Dark Age of Dogma* (Cambridge: Icon Books, 2004), 3–12.
77 See David C. Rapoport, "Comparing Militant Fundamentalist Movements," eds. Martin E. Marty and R. Scott Appleby, *Fundamentalisms and the State* (Chicago: University of Chicago Press, 1993), 445–6.
78 Chris Barker, *Cultural Studies: Theory and Practice* (London: Sage, 2012), 274.
79 As John Cogley wrote, "Anti-Catholicism has been called America's oldest and most abiding prejudice." John Cogley and Rodger Van Allen, *Catholic America: Expanded and Updated* (Kansas City: Sheed and Ward, 1986), 8.
80 See David Goldfield, *America Aflame: How the Civil War Created a Nation* (New York: Bloomsbury Press, 2011), 17–41.
81 See Chester Gillis, *Roman Catholicism in America* (New York: Columbia University Press, 1999), 68.
82 Richard Hofstadter, *Anti-Intellectualism in American Life* (New York: Alfred A. Knopf, 1966), 124.
83 See Cogley and Allen, *Catholic America*, 78–9; Chester Gillis, *Roman Catholicism in America* (New York: Columbia University Press, 1999), 231–2.
84 Pope Francis comments to journalists on plane returning from Africa (November 30, 2015). www.lifesitenews.com/news/pope-francis-attacks-fundamentalist-catholics-dismisses-condom-ban-as-unimp (Accessed March 26, 2016). See Arbuckle, *Fundamentalism at Home*, 97–124.
85 Cas Mudde, "The Populist Zeitgeist," *Government and Opposition*, vol. 39, no. 4 (2004): 543.
86 "The Threat from the Illiberal Left," *The Economist* (September 4, 2021), 7.
87 "The Threat From the Illiberal Left," 7.
88 See Jonathan Rauch, *The Constitution of Knowledge: A Defense of Truth* (Washington, DC: Brookings Institution Press, 2021), 10–14.
89 See Waleed Aly and Scott Stephens, "How Contempt Is Corroding Democracy," *Quarterly Essay*, no. 87 (2022): 1–71; Greg Lukainoff and Rikki Schlott, *The Cancelling of the American Mind: How Cancel Culture Undermines Trust, Destroys Institutions, and Threatens Us All* (New York: Simon and Schuster, 2023).
90 Ed. Michael Mann, *Macmillan Student Encyclopedia of Sociology* (London: Macmillan Press, 1983), 298; see also Margaret Canovan,

"Populism," eds. Adam Kuper and Jessica Kuper, *The Social Science Encyclopedia* (London: Routledge & Kegan Paul, 1985), 629–31.
91 An early example in the United States was Populist Party in the 1880s and 1890s, a grassroots, politically oriented alliance of agrarian reformers who were unhappy because of crop failures, falling prices, poor credit services, and assumed neglect by politicians in Washington, DC. See Chris Lehmann, *The Money Cult: Capitalism, Christianity, and the Unmaking of the American Dream* (Brooklyn, NY: First Melville House, 2016), 210–12.
92 Gideon Rachman, *The Age of the Strongman: How the Cult of the Leader Threatens Democracy Around the World* (London: The Bodley Press, 2021), 18.
93 David Goodhart, *The Road to Somewhere: The Populist Revolt and the Future of Politics* (London: Hurst, 2017), 74
94 Sergei Guriev and Daniel Treisman, *Spin Dictators: The Changing Face of Tyranny in the 21st Century* (Princeton: Princeton University Press, 2020), 18.
95 Mark Danner, "The Slow-Motion Coup," *The New York Review of Books* (October 6, 2022), 40; Trump, when president, refused to acknowledge the ongoing human tragedy of the pandemic in the nation; in a third wave of the virus the death toll continued to rise and the human costs to survivors and the nation as a whole are immeasurable. See Arbuckle, *The Pandemic and the People of God*, 95; Shana Kushner Gadarian, Sara Wallace Goodman, and Thomas B. Pepinsky, *Pandemic Politics: The Deadly Toll of Partisanship in the Age of COVID* (Princeton: Princeton University Press, 2022).
96 Jean M. Twenge and W. Keith Campbell, *The Narcissism Epidemic* (New York: Atria, 2013), 19.
97 See Christopher Lasch, *The Culture of Narcissism* (New York: Warner, 1991), and Rollo May, *The Cry of Myth*, op.cit., 110–24.
98 See Gideon Rachman, *The Age of the Strong Man: How the Cult of the Leader Threatens Democracy Around the World* (London: The Bodley Head, 2022), 1–24.
99 Recep Tayyip Erdogan quoted in *The Economist*, "Getting Off the Train," (February 6, 2016), 5. Regarding the tensions between populism and democracy see Benjamin Moffitt, *Populism* (Cambridge: Polity Press, 2020), 94–114.
100 See Jan-Werner Muller, www.nybooks.com/daily/2016/04/14/behind-new-german-right-afd?utm_medi (Accessed April 17, 2016).
101 See Michael Tomasky, "The Dangerous Election," *The New York Review of Books* www.nybooks.com/aricles/2016/03/24/the-dangerous-election/?utm_medium=e (Accessed March 4, 2016).
102 See Ruth Wodak, *The Politics of Fear: What Right-Wing Populist Discourses Mean* (London: SAGE, 2015), 4–6.
103 See Mark Danner, "The Grievance Artist," *The New York Review of Books* (November 2, 2023), 82.
104 "Conspiracy Thinking," *The Economist* (July 15, 2015), 31.

105 Mark Danner, "On the Election II," *The New York Review of Books* (November 10, 2016), 19.
106 Jill Lepore, *These Truths: A History of the United States* (New York: W.W. Norton, 2018), 782.
107 See Arbuckle, *Loneliness*, 67–8.
108 See Michael Tomasky, "Trump," *The New York Review of Books*, www.nybooks.com/articles/2015/09/24/trump/?utm_medium=email&utm_cam (Accessed December 14, 2015).
109 Quinta Jurecic, "Dispatches: Trump on Trial," *The Atlantic* (October, 2023), 15.
110 Tomasky, "Trump".
111 "Workers, Disunited," *The Economist* (August 19, 2017), 29. Among the groups present were: The League of the South, a group seeking a southern republic that would reject non-white culture and people; Vanguard America, one of several white supremacist organizations established after the presidential election of 2016; Radical Agenda, a fascist group that helped organize the march; Loyal Knights of the Klu Klux Klan; and the National Policy Institute, a group known for its use of the Nazi salute.
112 Robert G. Parkinson, *The Common Cause: Creating Race and Nation in the American Revolution* (Chapel Hill: University of North Carolina, 2016), 22.
113 *The Economist* comments: "Germany, Austria and Switzerland all imposed lockdowns before they had reached 60 deaths. By contrast, Britain already had 300 deaths by March 23rd, when its government ordered people to stay at home. This slow response allowed the virus to reach the entire country. . . . Sweden, which did not impose a lockdown at all, has suffered a similarly widespread epidemic." "How Speedy Lockdowns Save Lives," (July 4, 2020) (PDF).
114 See Geoffrey Wheatcroft, "The Opportunist Triumphant," *The New York Review of Books* (February 13, 2020), 32–5. Wheatcroft comments: "In October [2019], Johnson called for Britain 'to be released from the subjection of a parliament that has outlived its usefulness." 32; Dan Sabbagh, "Cultivating Conspiracy: How Boris Johnson Amplified the Far Right." *The Guardian*, www.theguardian.com/uk-news/2022/feb/08/cultivating-conspiracy-how-boris-johnson-amplified-the-far-right (Accessed March 19, 2023).
115 Martin Wolf, chief economics commentator of the *Financial Times* (UK), writes: "The rise of Trump, along with that of Boris Johnson in the UK, undermined the international credibility of the two countries and weakened Western cohesion. Above all, their demagogic approach to politics undermined the rule of law, the commitment to truth, and the credibility of international agreements, all fundamental underpinnings of liberal democracy. Outright despotism is the probable end point." *The Crisis of Democratic Capitalism*, xvii–xviii.
116 See "Why Governments Get It Wrong," *The Economist* (September 29, 2020), 9.

117 See Editorial, *The Tablet* (July 19, 2023), 2. See Arbuckle, *The Pandemic*, 88–9.
118 See Wolf, *The Crisis of Democratic Capitalism*, 35–7, 48–9; Pranab Bardhan, *A World of Insecurity: Democratic Disenchantment in Rich and Poor Countries* (Harvard: Harvard University Press, 2022); "African Politics: Losing Faith in Democracy," *The Economist* (October 7, 2023), 8.
119 Even Donald Trump claimed to have "absolute power" to decide when lockdowns should end, but he was quickly reminded that America's Constitution forbade it. "Covid-19 and Autocracy," *The Economist* (April 25, 2020), 48.
120 See Patrick Kingsley and Boryana Dzhambazova, "Lockdown Used as a Weapon to Repress Roma," *Times Digest* (July 7, 2020), 2.
121 See Sergei Guriev and Daniel Treisman, *Spin Dictators: The Changing Face of Tyranny in the 21st Century* (Princeton: Princeton University Press, 2022), 13–22.
122 See "Belarus's Bogus Election," *The Economist* (August 15, 2020), 41.
123 See "Covid-19 in the Balkans," *The Economist* (August 8, 2020), 39.
124 Vladimir Putin quoted by Rob Harris, "Fear and Loathing in Moscow: Putin Lays Out a Paranoid Vision of the World," *Sydney Morning Herald* (February 22, 2023), 14.
125 Matthew Specter and Varsha Venkatasubramanian, "'America First': Nationalism, Nativism, and the Fascist Question: 1880–2020," eds. Gavriel D. Rosenfeld and Janet Ward, *Fascism in America: Past and Present* (Cambridge: Cambridge University Press, 2023), 130.
126 Donald Trump cited by Marianne LeVine, "Trump Calls Political Enemies 'Vermin', echoing Dictators Hitler and Mussolini," *The Washington Post* (November 12, 2023) (PDF). See Thomas Byrne Edsall, *The Point of No Return: American Democracy at the Crossroads* (Princeton: Princeton University Press, 2023).
127 Tom Nichols, "Trump Crosses a Crucial Line," *The Atlantic Daily* (November 17, 2023) (PDF); see also Miles Taylor, *Blowback: A Warning to Save Democracy from the Next Trump* (New York: Atria, 2023), 70–88 and Geoff Eley, "What Is Fascism and Where Does It Come From?" Rosenfeld and Ward, *Fascism in America*, 66–71.
128 Zanny Minton Beddoes, "Democracy in Danger," *The Economist* (November 18–24, 2023), 7.
129 "America's House of Representatives Finally Has a Speaker," *The Economist* (October 26, 2023), 32.
130 Gavriel D. Rosenfeld and Janet Ward, "Introduction: Fascism in America: Past and Present," Rosenfeld and Ward, *Fascism in America*, 1.
131 Walter Brueggemann notes: "It is important to accent that something like 'God's preferential option for the poor' is deeply rooted in Israel's speech about God. The claim is not a belated, incidental addendum to Israel's ethical reflection, but belongs integrally and inalienably to Israel's core affirmation of the character of Yahweh." *Theology of the Old Testament: Testimony, Dispute, Advocacy* (Minneapolis: Fortress Press, 2005), 144.

132 A scriptural parable is a story about ordinary individuals and everyday events, but are recounted in a way that people in every century can identify with. Parables challenge readers to shape a world in which love and justice prevail in human relationships, a world of inner and outer conversion and reconciliation with one another and with their Creator. One of P.G. Wodehouse's characters remarks: "A parable is one of those stories in the Bible which sounds at first like a pleasant yarn but keeps something up its sleeves which pops up and leaves you flat." Cited by A.M. Hunter, *Interpreting the Parables* (London: SCM Press, 1960), 14.
133 Charles Taylor, *The Secular Age* (Cambridge: Cambridge University Press, 2007), 738.
134 Chris Marshall, "'Go and Do Likewise': The Parable of the Good Samaritan and the Challenge of Public Ethics," eds. Jonathan Boston, Andrew Bradstock and David Eng, *Ethics and Public Policy: Contemporary Issues* (Wellington: Victoria University Press, 2011), 53.
135 See C. Daniel Batson, "Attribution as a Mediator of Bias in Helping," *Journal of Personality and Social Psychology*, vol. 32, no. 3 (1975): 455–66; Hanokh Dagan, "In Defense of the Good Samaritan," *Michigan Law Review*, vol. 97, no. 5 (1999): 1115–200.
136 See Marshall, "Go and Do Likewise," 53.
137 See David K. Urion, *Compassion as a Subversive Activity* (Cambridge, MA: Cowley Publications, 2006), 48; John Swinton, *Raging with Compassion: Pastoral Responses to the Problem of Evil* (London: SCM Press, 2018).
138 See comments by Conor M. Kelly, "Everyday Solidarity: A Framework for Integrating Theological Ethics and Ordinary Life," *Theological Studies*, vol. 81, no. 2 (2020): 415–37.
139 Marcus Mescher, *Ethics of Encounter: Christian Neighbor Love as a Practice of Solidarity* (Maryknoll, NY: Orbis Books, 2020), 94–5.
140 David Hollenbach, *Common Good and Christian Ethics* (Cambridge: Cambridge University Press, 2002), 189.
141 Walter Brueggemann, *The Prophetic Imagination* (Minneapolis: Fortress Press, 1978), 49.
142 See Becker, *Escape From Evil*, 108–14.
143 See Amitav Acharya, "Hierarchies of Weakness: The Social Divisions That Hold Countries Back," *Foreign Affairs*, vol. 101, no. 4 (2022): 74–82.
144 See Yascha Mounk, *The People vs Democracy: Why Our Freedom Is in Danger and How to Save It* (Boston: Harvard University Press, 2020), 1–21; *The Economist*, "Covid-19: No Vaccine for Cruelty," (October 17, 2020), 9, 50–2.
145 Norris and Inglehart, *Cultural Backlash*, 464.

4 Conspiracy Theorizing and Magical Thinking
Is There a Connection?

> The twenty-first century is challenging any notion that politics can be free of magical thinking.... [P]opulist governments ... often eschew normal sources of scientific and academic authority in favour of conspiracy theories.
>
> (Francis Young)[1]

> Magical thinking expressed in conspiracy theories is alive and well, as recent insurrection events at the US Capitol have shown.
>
> (Susan Green)[2]

> It should be no surprise that occultism and conspiracy theories have connections and overlaps.
>
> (Michael Barkun)[3]

This chapter explains that:

- Truth can be obtained in two ways: through *logos* and *mythos*.
- Conspiracy theorizing and magical thinking belong to *mythos*.
- The sole criterion for truths in mythologies is that people believe them.
- Conspiracy theorizing and magical thinking are linked.
- Magical thinking is the ultimate evil as God is replaced by demons and associated forces.

There is a remarkable contemporary surge of interest in the connection between magic and conspiracy theorizing in Western societies among academics, particularly anthropologists, sociologists, and historians.[4] They are connected or overlap for two reasons: they both demand belief from their followers and both assume mystical manipulators lurking behind the scenes.

The aim of this chapter is to highlight this relationship in both premodern[5] and postmodern cultures. In premodern cultures the connection

DOI: 10.4324/9781003472162-5

is commonly quite evident but in modern industrialized cultures it is far less so. The scriptures condemn magical thinking and action. Magic here is understood as a collection of beliefs that have no foundation in established experimental sciences and associated disciplines.[6] It is expressed in two ways: magical thinking and action. The former is the belief that we can control the uncontrollable world.[7] The latter consists of practical rituals motivated by the belief that a desired result can be obtained through the manipulation of spiritual forces.[8]

Magical Thinking and Action Explained

Proposition 1: The fundamental core of magic is that it rests on empirically untested belief and that it is an effort at controlling the uncontrollable; the first aspect distinguishes it from science, the second from religion.[9]

The term "magical thinking" denotes a complex belief on the basis of which persons and groups may attempt to control their environment in such a way as to achieve their ends, the efficacy of such control being untested and in some cases untestable by the methods of empirical science. Since conspiracy theorizing refuses to be reality checked, it is also an example of magical thinking. *Magical action* is a secret ritual that is automatically expected to have the desired human consequences.[10] If a magical ritual fails to achieve its desired effect, it means that another secret ritual must be found. Magical beliefs and practices are followed by adherents with varying degrees of seriousness and involvement. Divination is a type of magic that tries to foretell the future by occult or supernatural means.

Proposition 2: A culture more or less adheres because of symbols, myths, and rituals.

Anyone who writes today on culture is confronted with a disheartening task. Anthropologists have never been able to agree on a single definition of culture. In 1952 researchers estimated that there were at least two hundred rival definitions of culture[11] and over subsequent decades the number of definitions has increased by more hundreds.

Edward Tylor first used a *modern* definition of culture in 1871: it is the "complex whole which includes knowledge, belief, art, morals, law, custom, and any other capabilities and habits acquired by man as a member of society."[12] There are two key aspects to his definition. First, culture comprises those human attributes that are learned and learnable and are therefore passed on socially and mentally, rather than biologically. Second, culture is in some sense a "complex whole"; order, unity, rationality, and harmony are key assumptions. Cultures are like the body of an animal. The purpose of each organ is to contribute to the unity and order of the whole body. So also in cultures. Institutions or social structures exist to maintain order and the survival of cultures. Individuals are so constrained, even coerced, by these structures that their behaviour has a certain social and cultural regularity. In brief, modern definitions of culture emphasize a type of 'billiard ball' model of cultures as separate, impenetrable units, passing with little or no change from one generation to the next in a quasi-automatic way, self-integrating to maintain order, resistant to external influences, homogeneous and devoid of internal dissent.[13]

Until the 1980s anthropologists commonly accepted the modern description of cultures. Yet, now in these postmodern times, it is clear that cultures simply do not fit this description.[14] Every culture is fragmented to some degree or other, internally contested, its borders permeable. There is no such thing as a "pure" culture. Never has been. Never will be. Cultures are hybrid, constantly interacting, mixing, and changing.[15] With globalization this process is intensifying so that happenings in one part of the world are being shaped by events developing many miles away and vice versa.[16] A postmodern definition of culture, therefore, is

> a pattern of meanings, encased in a network of symbols, narrative symbols, that is, myths and rituals, created over time by dominant groups, subcultures and individuals, as they struggle to achieve their identities in the midst of the competitive pressures of power and limited resources in a rapidly globalizing and fragmenting postmodern world, and instructing its adherents about what is considered to be the correct and orderly way to *feel*, *think*, and *behave*.[17]

This definition has several particular benefits. It emphasizes the power influences within cultures of dominant groups, subcultures, and individuals. The term "subculture" is a method of defining and honouring the particular design and identity of different interests or of a group of people within a larger collectivity. The term is a reminder that cultures are not homogenous, but commonly significantly fragmented.[18] In every subculture there is always an aspect, sometimes intensely obvious, of protest against the dominant culture of which it is part. The more people of the subculture feel threatened by the dominant group, the stronger and more vivid will be their symbols of protest and resistance.

The definition also highlights the fact that a culture (and its subcultures), through its symbols, myths, and rituals, shapes people's *emotional* responses to the world around them. In a culture people feel an affective sense of belonging, but also depending on the context, they can experience other emotions such as shame and anger. The comment by psychoanalyst Erich Fromm, therefore, is particularly incisive: "The fact that ideas have an emotional matrix is of the utmost importance because it is the key to understanding of the spirit of a culture."[19]

Proposition 3: There are two ways of obtaining truth: through mythos (i.e. myth) and logos. Magical thinking belongs to mythos;[20] conspiracy theories are a type of magical thinking that give particular meaning to those who believe them.

It has often been assumed that our premodern ancestors thought, spoke, and achieved truths through two important ways: *mythos* and *logos*, the former being by far the more common. *Logos* is the rational, pragmatic, objective, and scientific knowledge that permits people to function in the world. This "is rationalistic language. This is specific and empirical, and eventuates in logic."[21] The criteria for truths of *logos* are externally approved by solid evidence of rational thinking. Since the Enlightenment it is commonly and falsely thought that Westerners no longer need *mythos* because it is assumed that everything that exists can be logically and scientifically measured.[22] If it cannot be measured it does not exist. Therefore, as myths cannot be measured, the truths they contain for their believers do not exist. Given the widespread mythological resurgence of nationalism, religion, and fundamentalism, this claim that the world is becoming increasingly secular or rationalized, that is, that Westerners do not need *mythos*, has proved a dangerous fallacy.[23]

Magical thinking and action, which can include conspiracy theorizing, belong to the world of *mythos*, or myths. Now to explain *mythos*. Contrary to popular belief, myths are not fairy tales. Myths and mythologies (collections of interrelated myths) anthropologically are narrative symbols; that is, they are emotionally charged stories that draw people together at the deepest level of group life, and which they live by and for. A myth is a story or tradition that claims to reveal in an imaginative way a fundamental *belief* or *truth* about the world and human life. All social groups, for example, will have founding myths that are the ultimate binding forces of identity and hope in the future. The founding myth of the United States is the new Israel born out of a new Exodus, the new "Promised Land," where democracy will protect its citizens from the corrupting forces of monarchs and dictators.[24]

Myths are thus value-impregnated *beliefs* that hold a society together, even though people may not be consciously aware of this. They are stories that claim to articulate in, an imaginative way, fundamental truths about human life. These truths are regarded as authoritative by those who believe them. *That is, unlike truths in logos the sole criterion for truths in mythologies is that people believe them.* But without myths people do not have any reason to be or to act. Myths, Peter Berger writes, have the power to lift people "above their captivity in the ordinary, and attain powerful visions of the future, and become capable of collective actions to realize such visions." A myth has the ability to transcend "both pragmatic and theoretical rationality, while at the same time it strongly affects them."[25] Myths differ from paradigms. The latter are *cognitive* frameworks created to describe in a comprehensible way complex realities; unlike myths, they lack any emotive quality.[26]

By mythically defining and structuring the world, the human person and group are able to grasp to some degree or other the regions beyond human control which influence well-being and destiny. Like sacred icons, myths are the medium of revelation handed down from the heroes of the past,[27] so they are not to be lightly discarded or questioned. Like all symbols, myths can evoke deep emotional responses. No matter how committed we are to deepen our grasp of the meaning of myths, they still remain somewhat ambiguous and mysterious, because they attempt to express what can never be fully explained. The more we try the more we discover new and unexpected meanings in myths. To summarize:

- Myths are at the heart of every culture. Emotionally embedded in them are a culture's fundamental values and assumptions about life.[28] They are the glue that binds people together, giving them a sense of identity and purpose. They claim to reveal in an imaginative and symbolic way fundamental truths about the world and human life;[29] *they are efforts to explain what usually is beyond empirical observation.* Myths are as indispensable in our contemporary world as in the past. They drive every one of us. They are the source of meaning in our lives.
- Myths can be likened to knowledge hidden in the DNA of a cell, or the program technology of a computer; myths are the cultural templates or invisible blueprints of the heart and mind, the programmes that frame the way we interpret the world and how we must act.[30] When this emotional programming is destroyed for whatever reason, we are in chaos.
- Magical thinking and conspiracy theorizing belong to *mythos* and thus give meaning to their believers. *Mythos* seeks to articulate what cannot be stated in simple logical and scientific language. That is, myth does not attempt to be 'factual' or rational, and so it cannot be demonstrated or verified.
- Unlike truths in *logos* the sole criterion for truths in mythologies is that people believe them. Conspiracy theories and magic are mythologically connected for two reasons: they both demand *belief* from their followers and both assume mystical manipulators behind the scenes.
- *Logos*, with its emphasis on rational thinking alone, cannot possibly address issues of ultimate meaning.[31] But *mythos*, unlike *logos*, answers

issues of ultimate meaning; they respond to the need we have for the sense of purpose in our lives. As Rollo May writes: "Whereas empirical language refers to objective facts, *myth refers to the quintessence of human experience, the meaning and significance of human life*. The whole person speaks to *us*, not just to our brain."[32]

Proposition 4: The scope of magical rituals is highly elastic; they can include, for example, rituals of curing, divining, casting spells through witchcraft or sorcery, transforming the weather, making crops prosper or fail, summoning spirits and demons, and conspiracy theorizing to account for mystifying events.[33]

People believe that if they have the right magical ritual they can cause harm to others and protect themselves. Witchcraft accusations publicly identify the causes of personal or group calamities.[34] They brand innocent people as witches and subject them to violence, even at times death.[35] Historians acknowledge that gossip was a fundamental factor in the fostering of social and political turmoil that resulted in the magic-inspired witchcraft accusations and trials in seventeenth-century colonial New England.[36]

Proposition 5: Ritual is the repetitive spontaneous or prescribed symbolic use of bodily movement and gesture to express and articulate meaning;[37] *conspiracy theories are rituals of passage especially in times of personal and cultural crises.*

Ritual action occurs within a *social context*, where there is possible or real tension/conflict in social relations, and efforts are undertaken to resolve or hide it. In other words, ritual is "a performance, planned or improvised, that effects a transition from everyday life to an alternative context within which the everyday is transformed."[38]

"Rites of passage" is a term first used by anthropologist Arnold Van Gennep (1873–1957) to describe particular transformative rituals that assist people or groups to transit safely from one social status to another.[39] The crossing over to a new status can be full of uncertainty and tensions. Hence the name rites of passage, that is, rituals that aim to effect secure changes in threatening times. They are *initiation* rituals because they assist individuals or groups to make the transition from one social status to a new identity, as well as assisting society to accept significant changes in the status of members. Examples of rites of passage are those that accompany birth, marriage, initiation into adulthood, sickness to health, employment and retirement, and appointment to or departure from political or religious offices.

The present world is in a dangerous liminal period. People are daily reminded of national and international tensions. Cultures and individuals need rituals to help them transit safely through these liminal periods. It is a time for *rites of passage*.[40] Magical rituals, including conspiracy theories, are *rites of passage* because they are instruments whose purpose for individuals or groups is to change or transform a fear-evoking situation where control is lacking to one of control.[41]

Proposition 6: Leaders of magical rituals need to be deeply imbued with the mythology of the culture in which they practice. Depending on the cultural context they can be variously termed witches, sorcerers, shamans, witch-doctors, diviners, even populist leaders in modern times. They have the ability to cause evil or/and identify its sources claiming to relieve the evil through rituals and conspiracy theorizing.

Ritual guides aim to pilot clients through the chaos of uncertainties to the new status, reminding them that they have to learn new behaviours and abandon former ones. In the process there is always a period of ambiguity and risk. Clients must grapple with a threefold tension: the urge to escape nostalgically to a past status, *or* to remain paralysed by doubts, *or* to move forward into the unknown to obtain a fresh status. Clients need the guidance of a new transforming narrative, for example conspiracy theories, containing values to form the foundation of the new status. Will clients choose to accept advice? Will they give up their old ways of acting? If not, they fail to be initiated into a new status.

Ritual leaders concretize by their behaviour the idea that a new world of control *is* possible. Myth specialist Joseph Campbell describes the ritual leader in this way. He or she is a "hero" who "ventures forth from the world of common day into a region of supernatural wonder; fabulous forces are encountered and a decisive victory is won. The hero comes back from this mysterious adventure with the power to bestow boons on his fellow man [*sic*]."[42] The ritual leader is considered a hero who has visited, and been converted to the vision of a new world of control.[43] Their behaviour mirrors this interior transformation. Clients who are believers, recognizing that their leader carries within themselves the vision of their journey's end, are drawn to experience the same action-oriented conversion. In brief:

- Magic claims to control the uncontrollable through rituals that rest on empirically untested beliefs.
- Conspiracy theories are a type of magical thinking that gives particular meaning to those who believe them.
- Magical rituals, including conspiracy theorizing, are rites of passage by which people believe they can safely transit from situations of no control to one of control.

- Individuals become ritual leaders on their own authority or are assigned this task by others because it is assumed they have special knowledge to do so.
- If magical rituals fail to work for believers, it is because the wrong rituals have been selected; new rituals must be chosen

Magic and Conspiracy Thinking in Premodernity[44]

Premodern cultures are widely found in traditional Asia, Africa, parts of North, Middle, South America, and the South Pacific. In these cultures the world of humans and spirits is one and the same;[45] good and bad spirits constantly interact with humans in the same world. Thus the enlisting of bad spirits by humans for evil reasons through sorcery and witchcraft magical beliefs and rituals remains unquestioned.[46] A sorcerer's ability to cause mischief depends on their ability to manipulate powers extrinsic to himself. A witch, on the other hand, is believed to cause mischief such as sickness or death for others simply by staring at them or willing evil on them; they possess powers – inherited or acquired – as an intrinsic part of their personality.[47]

The fear of being accused of witchcraft and sorcery can shame people to act appropriately according to cultural norms (see *Proposition 9*, Chapter 1).[48] However, accusations can cause incalculable violence to innocent people.[49] Magical practices in all their forms, which as elements of premodern cultures had co-existed for centuries alongside Christianity, were transformed in the European imagination into a collage of witches' sabbaths, devil worship, and cannibalistic feasts, resulting in the terrible witch trials of the sixteenth and seventeenth centuries. Hundreds of thousands perished.[50] In contemporary premodern cultures in which witchcraft and sorcery accusations continue to flourish, innocent people can be subjected to violence, even at times death, because they are branded as witches. For example, in parts of India, people accused of witchcraft "are burned, hacked to death, typically by mobs made up by their neighbours and, sometimes, their own relatives."[51]

Identifying Sources of Evil: Witch-hunting Through Conspiracy Thinking

Good health in premodern cultures exists when people live in harmony with each other, their gods, or spirits. Health can be recovered through the use of a wide variety of folk medicines, but these are useless if social relationships and events are not renewed, and evil spirits ritually ejected, for it is they which are the primary cases of illness and sickness. Since sickness reflects the social circumstances of the individual, it cannot be reduced to one physical cause such as a germ; rather, it is a form of evil that has complex social implications and causes.

People accept that there are immediate and rational causes for misfortune; for example, heart attacks can cause death. For every misfortune there is always a physical or natural cause. However, a further and far more important question, namely "*Why* is *this* person sick with cancer at *this* time and in *this* place?" or "*Why* did *this* person die with cancer?" or "*Why* did my crops fail?" must be answered in different ways. *Who* is responsible? The answer: some particular person or persons are witches or sorcerers conspiring to cause harm. They must be identified and punished. The identification of *who* is responsible constitutes a *conspiracy theory*. That is, a conspiracy theory is created in the process of identifying malevolent witches or sorcerers. People who are thought to threaten the existing power structures are the most vulnerable. For example, in the Middle Ages through to the seventeenth century, theories concentrated on women; they were assumed to be weaker and consequently more vulnerable to the wiles of the devil.

> Authorities typically singled out women who deviated from religiously established norms for females. . . . [They] in particular were considered threats to social purity because of cultural assumptions about their sexuality and because anomalous (i.e. independent) women were perceived as dangerous and disruptive.[52]

Examples of Premodern Conspiracy Thinking

The following are several examples of conspiracy theorizing which often have unfortunate consequences for innocent people.

One day when I was tramping through the bush in the Southern Highlands, Papua New Guinea, I came across a young man with a severe arm injury resting in a hut built far from the village. I offered to arrange for transport to a medical centre, but my suggestion was quickly rejected by his father, who commented:

> If we take him away he will surely die, because someone will work more sorcery on him. The government medical men can do nothing for him, unless we find out who has worked sorcery on him. It is surely a sorcerer who wants to harm him and our village because of something someone in our clan has done wrong.

His son's arm, already dangerously infected, was due, he knew, to an accident, but its ultimate cause was surely the result of someone working sorcery and wanting to inflict social disruption in the village. Unless the sorcerer could be discovered and the right magic used to counter the evil, the boy's arm would not heal and he would surely die. The father would not change his mind. "We are using secret ritual to identify the sorcerer," he said. "He will be speared or their family must make retribution."

In Papua New Guinea the Tolai people assume that sorcery causes a headache and insanity.[53] Anthropologist Garry Trompf commented on urban life in Port Moresby, capital of Papua New Guinea: "Certain deaths and instances of insanity among senior public servants . . . have even been attributed to sorcery by the broad consensus view of their national colleagues."[54] Among the aboriginal Yolngu community in Australia, when there is a death it is taken for granted that sorcery is the cause.[55] Someone must be identified and punished.

The Azande people in Africa people are very aware that there are natural reasons for sickness or death, but they need additional explanations, that is conspiracy theories, to account for what has happened. If a person enters the bush and is killed by an elephant, his relatives want to know why this happened. They acknowledge that the terrible mortal injuries caused death, but they need to know why *this* man was killed by *this* elephant at *this* particular moment and in *this* specific place, and not someone else. The answer is simple: he was the object of witchcraft or sorcery by a person to be identified and disciplined. Hence, for every occurrence of sickness or adversity, there are two fundamental questions, namely *how* and *why* it happened; the second question is answered in terms of witchcraft or sorcery and the guilty person must be discovered and punished.[56]

Cargo Cults is the name given to millenarian movements in Melanesia (i.e. Papua New Guinea, Solomon Islands, Vanuatu), in the South Pacific.[57] They centre on a belief that special knowledge of rituals and observances decreed by the ancestors will suddenly bring the people material rewards, notably manufactured goods, and a better, even paradisaical life (i.e. locally called "cargo"). The malevolent white colonizers, according to local conspiracy theorists, have stolen the secret knowledge from the ancestors who traditionally are the source of prosperity. The "cargo" message of messianic leaders is: ritually repudiate the past by dramatically destroying crops and other goods as the pre-condition for the coming of the "new heaven" of prosperity.

One example of the ritual is the clearing ground for airstrips, and surrounding them with bamboo landing lights, to receive the prophesized aircraft containing the cargo. Rituals like this will allow the ancestors to use their special knowledge to overcome the Europeans. Blacks will become whites, and whites will turn Black, and the white domination will finish. When the rituals fail there is great despondency, but new leaders emerge claiming that their predecessors did not have the "right rituals," so the cycle of destruction and hollow promises of impressive prosperity begin all over again. The cargo cults and their associated conspiracy theories are a magical indigenous response to traumatic contact with the Western world.

Maori people in New Zealand traditionally believed any failure of health is due to malignant spirits.[58] In contemporary times when the cause of sickness is not easily understood or existing medical treatment is unsuccessful, Maoris often speak of *mate Maori* (i.e. "Maori sickness"). The chief causes of *mate* Maori are commonly attributed especially to sorcery. Anthropologist Joan Metge wrote that the fear "of sorcery is dormant most of the time, becoming dominant only under stress in the face of the unaccountable. A diagnosis of sorcery usually involves attributing responsibility to some particular person . . . known to envy or have been offended by the victim."[59] Once sorcery is diagnosed and neutralized the conspiracy theory is that "sorcery recoils on the originator,"[60] whose sickness or death is considered to prove guilt.

In Samoan society, noted Ineke Lazar, culture-bound disorders (*ma'i aitu*) can include a severe form of hysterical psychosis, other neurotic symptoms, and certain physiological conditions. A common complaint, she found, in the Los Angeles Samoan community is that, in the words of her informants, "Samoan illnesses do not show up on X-rays. So, the doctor does not know what to do." The people turn to traditional Samoan ritual therapists specializing in *aitu* ("spirit") related illnesses, who use what they believe is spirit medicine. They must find out where the spirit comes from and why it is troubling the living.[61] The answer will constitute a conspiracy theory. For example, it was reported in 1971 that in a contemporary Samoan village a man had become deranged and was considered to be possessed by an *aitu* ("spirit"). A family member acknowledged that he had not properly cared for his aunt when she was alive. The extended family met and concluded that her *aitu* was punishing them. They then ritually pushed a pipe into her grave and filled it with boiling water and the man was restored to good health.[62]

Ritual Leaders: Creators of Conspiracy Thinking

In traditional cultures there are a variety of ritual specialists, shamans, or diviners, and methods to discern precisely which spirit or person is causing the evil, the reasons why, and the necessary remedies.[63] They, often together with families of people who are suffering, create the relevant conspiracy theory that makes sense of particular disasters.

In the African Azande mythology oracles are used to identify the witches responsible for problems. In the termite oracle, for example, two sticks are placed in a termite mound for a day; the answer is found by noting which stick was eaten first. The termite oracle is considered to be less reliable than the intricate and costly poison oracle which needs to be used to tackle the identified witch and to begin the vengeance process when death is involved.⁶⁴ The renowned anthropologist Edward Evans-Pritchard argues that the Azande people are thinking magically quite logically within a closed system typical of conspiracy theorizing: "Within the limits set by these patterns . . . they reason excellently in the idiom of their beliefs, *but they cannot reason outside, or against, their beliefs because they have no other idiom in which to express their thoughts.*"⁶⁵

Conspiracy theorizing is an integral quality of Shamanism, the term for an intricate mixture of magical and ethno-medical beliefs and practices found among cultures in Asia, Africa, and aboriginal America. Shamans can use spiritual powers to counter the influence of enemies and cause or cure disease. While sickness may have several causes, the most important is due to the loss of the soul through evil forces. The shaman's skill, exercised through a trancelike state, is to find the missing soul in some hidden section of the cosmic world and restore it to the sick person.⁶⁶ A shaman is not considered to be an abnormal person but is often a central figure in a culture: "Not only are they responsible for curing and the magical protection of society, but they are regarded as repositories of valued cultural and mythological knowledge."⁶⁷

Magic and Conspiracy Thinking in Postmodernity

> Politics always contains an element of the occult, mystical and magical; the recent breakdown of the political inhibitions of the 1990s and 2000s simply made these elements more apparent.
>
> (Francis Young)⁶⁸

As explained in *Proposition 3*, the Enlightenment falsely denied the crucial role of mythology in our lives, and therefore the possibility of magical thinking; all human actions could be rationalized.⁶⁹ Yet the reverence for magical beliefs and practices in its various forms significantly continues today in the modern world though they may be more concealed than in premodern cultures.⁷⁰

Niall Ferguson comments:

> The advance of science led to a decline not only of magical thinking but also of religious belief and observance. As G.K. Chesterton foresaw, this had the unintended consequences of creating spaces in people's minds for new forms of magical thinking. *Modern societies are highly susceptible to surrogate religions and magic, leading to new forms of irrational activity that, on close inspection, are quite similar to pre-1700 behaviors.*⁷¹

Andrew Greely reflecting in 1993 on contemporary US Catholicism writes:

> My preliminary analysis . . . persuades me that both the religion and superstition survive and that indeed we may have a lot more in common with medieval peasants than we had thought. We live longer than they did and have far better medical care available, but they were probably no more religious than we are and we no less superstitious than they were.[72]

Omens, Charms, and Astrology

Postmodernity has certainly not killed off magical thinking. For example, there are beliefs in lucky amulets and charms, palmistry, astrology, and witchcraft. All may significantly influence people's worldviews.[73] An American survey in 1990 found that 25 per cent of the population believe in astrology; likewise, a Canadian study found that 34 per cent of respondents are committed to astrology, and 88 per cent consult their horoscopes at least monthly.[74] Astrology, a form of divination, involves the forecasting of earthly and human events through the observation and interpretation of the fixed stars, the sun, the moon, and the planets. Believers claim that an understanding of the influence of the planets and stars on earthly events allows them to predict the destinies of individuals, groups, and nations. Though often declared to be a science throughout its history, astrology is a form of magic.

Magical Thinking and Conspiracy Theorizing

More seriously is the impact of magical thinking, as expressed in conspiracy theorizing, on decision-making in the public arena. Historian Francis Young concludes:

> Politics always contains an element of the occult, mystical and magical; the recent breakdown of the political inhibitions of the 1990s and 2000s simply made these elements more apparent.[75] . . . The twenty-first century is challenging any notion that politics can be free of magical thinking . . . [P]opulist governments . . . often eschew normal sources of scientific and academic authority in favour of conspiracy theories.[76]

Eric Kurlander, in his classic study of the influence of magical thinking and conspiracy theorizing on the rise of Nazism, warns of the dangers of such thinking in contemporary politics:

As in Germany, a century ago, a renaissance in supernatural reasoning, shadowy conspiracy theories, extraterrestrial powers, and the omnipresence of a hostile ethno-religious other has begun to correlate with illiberal political and ideological convictions, influencing national elections, domestic social policies, and matters of war and peace. This phenomenon is evident globally, whether in the emergence of nativist and neo-fascist ("alt-right") groups across the United States or in the exponential spread and politicization of fundamentalist Islam.... The reality is that every culture has its own supernatural imaginary which can, in times of crisis, begin to displace more empirically grounded ... arguments.[77]

As I have explained, conspiracy theorizing is a type of magical mythological thinking; it is a belief that a group of people are secretly plotting to harm someone or achieve something. Conspiracy thinkers believe that they alone have secret knowledge of what is to happen or what has happened, even though there is no rational or historical foundation for the clandestine knowledge. The secret knowledge which has been deliberately hidden by evil forces has now become available to a select group. It has the above-average potential to cause harm to a significant number of people while benefiting others.

The magical qualities of conspiracy theories in modern societies may be overt, or unlike their counterparts in premodern culture, they are more commonly covert. They are made to look plausible to modern thinkers who would normally shun anything that looks like magic; when the magical quality is masked, the theories are presented as though they are rationally and/or historically accurate, which is not the case.[78] Recent anthropological research illustrates this point. Peter Geschiere compared African witch-doctors with modern political spin-doctors, as used by the British prime minister Tony Blair and the American president Bill Clinton. The spin-doctors may not have been aware that they were manipulating magic as such, but they were using emotional practices that aimed to operate in a magical way.[79] The following examples illustrate how magical thinking and conspiracy theorizing can be connected in modern cultures.

Nazism

Magical beliefs and practices were intermittently rooted out, suppressed, and outlawed by the Nazis. At the same time, however, they drew upon a wide variety of occult practices and esoteric sciences in order to acquire power and shape propaganda and policy aimed at bolstering their conspiracy theories of Germany as a racial utopia and the Jews as racially inferior.[80] Alfred Rosenberg, the influential Nazi intellectual, confidently proclaimed in 1941:

> The success of National Socialism, the unique appearance of the Fuhrer, has no precedence in German history. . . . The consequences of these historic and unprecedented political occurrences is that many Germans, due to their proclivity for the romantic and the mystical, indeed the occult, came to understand the success of National Socialism in this fashion.[81]

Nazi leadership was obsessed by the occult and no mass political movement in history has so consciously steeped itself in occult beliefs and practices such as astrology, mythical folklore, fringe science, and the paranormal. Rudolf Hess, Hitler's deputy, employed a personal astrologer. Heinrich Himmler was extreme in his occult obsessions. He even established the SS Witches Division[82] to gather evidence of witch trials and wizardry, based on the notion that these represented an ancient Germanic religion persecuted and wiped out by a cruel Judeo-Christian inquisition. The German Navy, the SS, and Goebbels' Propaganda Ministry all employed astrologers to gain military intelligence and organize psychological warfare.

Marxian Dialectic Theory

Marxist mythology originated in reaction to the violence of industrialism in Europe and promised people an egalitarian utopia. It offered a coherent belief system based on the Enlightenment's assumption of human perfectibility and the pseudo-science of economic determinism. The Marxian dialectic, a conspiracy theory that decrees the ultimate destruction of capitalism, has covert magical qualities. History is ideologically governed by universal laws; according to this theory, a society moves inexorably through a series of stages, with the transition between stages being irreversibly driven by the class struggle. This is a magical assumption that has no empirically tested foundations. The magical qualities of Marxism are concealed by the façade of intellectualism. The British-Hungarian intellectual Michael Polanyi (1891–1976), drawing on Evans-Pritchard's research among the African Azande people, commented that Marxism and Freudian theory was also closed, circular systems which prevented their followers from seeing the inconsistencies so clear to outsiders.[83]

McCarthyism

Consider the conspiracy theory that fuelled anti-communist McCarthyism in the United States in the 1950s. Senator Joseph McCarthy claimed that dozens of American communists had penetrated the administration, some at the highest levels, and stole scientific and political secrets. The timing was just right. McCarthy rose to notoriety when the fear of communism still raged, thanks to the Soviet Union's acquisition of the atomic bomb, the Communist Party's takeover of China, and the start of the Korean War. And McCarthy had just the "right" qualities to be the ritual leader of the anti-communist campaign: an extraordinary disregard for proven facts; a menacing personality; and his ability to brand the entire American elite establishment with communist infiltration, from Harvard University to Hollywood and the army. Whoever dared to question McCarthy's unfounded accusations risked being themselves branded communists.[84] McCarthyism responded to the need of people to control the fear-evoking world around them. The magical element in McCarthyism was covert but nonetheless real for its devotees. McCarthy's raging witch-hunting became a healing ritual that reassured his *believing* followers that they were at last being protected from an evil of frightening proportions. They refused to accept evidence to the contrary. His groundless ritual of scapegoating automatically and magically quieted their fears.

QAnon Conspiracy Theory

Anthropologist Susan Greenwood uncovered a magical mode of thought at the heart of the QAnon conspiracy theory. It influenced the insurrection of January 6, 2021, against the Capitol in Washington, DC, and it was directly encouraged by Donald Trump.[85] Symbols of QAnon iconography were common on the insurrectionists. Flags were flying with QAnon slogans boldly engraved on them. Greenwood focuses her analysis on a central QAnon supporter in insurgency, Juke Angeli (also known as Jacob Chansley, Loan, or Yellowstone Wolf), a decorated, former ex-naval storekeeper seaman apprentice. The magical qualities of the conspiracy theory are startlingly visible evident in Angeli's dress and body tattoos: pictured as a QAnon shaman, he was clothed in furs, face paint, and a horned helmet. Greenwood explains the symbols and their political implications. For example, the body tattoos originate from

> the Nordic mythological tradition, Mjolnir, the hammer of the thunder god Thor is a symbol of blessing and a weapon of protection against the forces of evil . . . Thor guards Asgard, the land of the gods, against the giants. . . . [The] Nordic symbol covering Angeli's heart is the stylized image of Yggdrasil, the cosmic tree containing nine worlds of intercommunication between gods and humans through the medium of myth.[86]

Fascism

Fascism is an authoritarian, nationalistic political movement that arises, like Nazism, out of particular experiences of social and economic chaos. Examples are: Italy under Benito Mussolini between 1922 and 1945; the Spanish Falange; Chile under General Pinochet; Iraq under Saddam Hussein; Russia under Vladimir Putin; Turkiye under Recep Tayyip Erdogan; Hungary under Viktor Orban; and now Donald Trump, with identifiable fascist qualities (see Chapter 3). Historian Roger Griffin argues that the distinctive element in fascist movements is to be found in a common mythic core from the Enlightenment: "the vision of the (perceived) crisis of the nation as betokening the birth-pangs of a new order."[87] The nation has been corrupted through the rationalism of modernity and its democratic values and can be regenerated provided citizens are prepared to give themselves totally to the state; if necessary, they must sacrifice their individual existence to the struggle against external and internal conspiring malevolent forces of degeneration that have brought the nation to disaster. At the heart of the state, however, is the cult of the male leader, the all-powerful leader to whom all must submit. Equipped with magical powers, bolstered by conspiracy theories, he will lead the nation to a new youthfulness provided the old order is destroyed.

Brexit

Britain, in 2016, voted with a narrow margin to leave the European Union (EU), the event that came to be called "Brexit." The extremist campaign on both sides of the issue bitterly divided the country leaving little middle ground.[88] Francis Young comments that "just as the most entrenched supporters on both sides of the Brexit debate have become vulnerable to magical thinking, so partisans on both sides showed themselves willing to believe conspiracy theories, ready to accuse opponents of 'treason' on a daily basis."[89] The radical nationalistic and anti-immigrant crusade backing Brexit was noted for its false claims about the positive advantage of leaving the EU, despite the fact these claims contradicted economic and political realities. The ritual of voting for Brexit would magically return sovereignty and prosperity to Britain. Pro-Brexit voters, however, were warned to use their own pens when casting ballots because the spy agency MI5 would erase the pencil marks on their ballots.[90] *The Economist*, reflecting on the resulting malaise evoked by this conspiracy theorizing, declared: "Worst of all, it has infected British politics with a destructive strain of magical thinking." It also warned those who wish to re-unite with the EU not to "succumb to hocus-pocus if they think that the split can be simply undone." It "will take time, hard work and realism,"[91] not the escape into magical thinking and conspiracy theorizing.

The Economist later reported that at the Tory party conference "A cabinet full of former accountants and management consultants attempted to peddle lines from online conspiracies." For example, "the environment secretary . . . claimed without basis that Labour would introduce a meat tax, noting that Sir Keir Starmer, the opposition leader, doesn't eat meat."[92]

Neoliberalism[93]

The economic model of neoliberalism (or often termed neocapitalism, market capitalism, market economics, neoclassical capitalism, market liberalism)[94] asserts that profit is the sole measure of value and the economic profession serves as its priesthood.[95] Societies, once freed from the restraints of governments and the costly welfare services for the poor, will flourish economically and socially for the benefit of all. The primary task of governments is to support individual initiatives in commerce.[96] Believers claim that provided neoliberalist rituals are adhered to, the new millenarian age will automatically follow.

But the model is based on conspiracy and magical thinking. The poor do not benefit. Neoliberalist mythology accepts the conspiracy theory of Social Darwinist, namely that the poor are what they are because of their own fault; welfare services make their poverty worse, so they must be reduced.[97] The poor are to be scapegoated and demonized. As a model it has been severely condemned for the harm it has caused people, but still it has its devotees who remain believers in its magical rituals. Its proponents are modern-day witch-doctors, playing on people's anxieties as snake oil, identifying dissenters as "evil doers," "destroyers of the common good."[98] Pope Francis comments:

> [Neoliberalism] simply reproduces itself by resorting to the *magic* theories of "spillover" or "trickle[down]" . . . as the only solution to societal problems. There is little appreciation of the fact that the alleged "spillover" does not resolve the inequality that gives rise to new forms of violence threatening the fabric of society.[99] . . . Everything comes under the laws of competition and the survival of the fittest, where the powerful feed upon the powerless. . . . Masses of people find themselves excluded . . . without work, without possibilities.[100]

Moreover, the rising economic insecurity and social deprivation among the left-behinds of neoliberalism have fuelled populist resentment against the model in the United States, Britain, and the West in general. It has encouraged authoritarian populist leaders, such as Donald Trump and promoters of Brexit, to feed on this resentment.[101] Prior to the Covid-19 pandemic crisis, Cambridge University professor of economics Paul

Collins, reflecting on the failure of neoliberal policies in America so evident in the global economic crisis of 2008–9, writes in 2019:

> In America, the emblematic heart of capitalism, half of the 1980s generation are absolutely worse off than the generation of their parents at the same age. For them, capitalism is not working. . . . Anxiety, anger and despair have shredded people's political allegiances, their trust in government and even their trust in each other.[102]

The onslaught of the pandemic further proved the economic magic wrong but the conspiracy-based model still has believers. In looking at the distressing penchant for magical cures to financial crises, one is reminded of David Hume's intuition: "In proportion as a man's course of life is governed by accident, we always find that he increases in superstition."[103]

Scriptural Critique

The Bible never states that magic such as sorcery or witchcraft is fake but affirms that they are helpless against the power of God.[104] Magical thinking and actions are ultimate evils because they dare to substitute God with demons; this is why the biblical language against magic in all its forms is so vigorously uncompromising.

Old Testament

> I am the Lord your God . . . you shall have no other gods before me.
> (Exod 20:2, 3)

The perspective of ancient Judaism towards witchcraft and sorcery appears to have been similar to that of many tribal cultures described by anthropologists.[105] Witches, sorcerers, and diviners were regarded with trepidation and suspicion, being associated with the idolatrous enemies of Israel: "No one shall be found among you who makes a son or daughter pass through fire or who practices divination, or is a soothsayer or an augur, or a sorcerer, or one who casts spells. . . . For whoever does these things is abhorrent to the Lord" (Deut 18:10, 10).[106] Deuteronomic theology demands that there is only one sovereign God; Israelites must not accept or defer to other arbitrary spiritual powers.[107] The prophets condemned magic as a depravity for which God will chastise the Israelites: "Do not let the prophets and the diviners who are among you deceive you, and do not listen to the dreams that they dream" (Jer 29:9). Ezekiel censured the sorceresses who thought they were able to control people by magical practices, but the power of God would instead triumph (Ezek 13:18–23).

New Testament

You foolish Galatians. Who has bewitched you?

(Gal 3:1)

Incidents

In the New Testament there are two incidents concerning magicians. They strongly reaffirm the Old Testament condemnations of anything magical. The first is the action of Simon who held people awe-struck in Samaria (Acts 8:9–11). He was baptized by Philip (Acts 8–13), after which he was no less astonished by Philip's signs and wonders and was filled with such envy that when Peter arrived Simon sought to obtain a similar power by a financial deal, which Peter vigorously repudiated: "Repent . . . of this wickedness" (Acts 8:22). Elymas is the second magician to be condemned for his actions: "You son of the devil, you enemy of all righteousness, full of deceit and villainy, you will not stop making crooked the straight paths of the Lord?" (Acts 13:10). Paul caused him to be struck with temporary blindness. He had to warn converts against sorcery: "those do such things will not inherit the kingdom of God" (Gal 5:20).[108] In the Book of Revelation sorcery is included in the list of odious vices (Rev 9:21; 21:8; 22:15).

Faith Imperative

Faith in Jesus Christ is necessary in order to resist magical thinking, behaviour, and conspiracy theorizing: "By faith we understand that the worlds were prepared by the word of God, so that what is seen was made from things that are not visible" (Heb 11:3). Faith in the person of Jesus Christ and his mission alone must guide all our thoughts and actions: "let us run with perseverance the race that is set before us, looking to Jesus the pioneer and perfecter of our faith, who for the sake of the joy that was set before him endured the cross, disregarding its shame" (Heb 12:1-2). In Hebrew times God was one with those who suffered, and in Christ, there is total identification. Now Jesus himself is the poor one, born in a stable (Luke 2:7), the one killed for the people (Luke 24:20).

The conspiracy theorists of Christ's day condemn the sick and poor as society's polluted or unclean, scapegoated to the boundaries of the community. To speak to them or touch them renders others unclean and unloved by God, but faith in Christ means that God especially loves them. Such attitudes and behaviour are contrary to the mission of Christ. In publicly proclaiming his mission, Jesus asserts that he is the one promised in Isaiah (Isa 58:6; 61:12); he is the one to bring good news to the poor, release the captives and the oppressed, and give sight to the blind (Luke 4:16-21). Jesus wants the poor to be recognized as the heirs of God; he is the Messiah of the poor ((Luke 4:18). This is revolutionary; people see it as such and do not want to hear anymore because his words go against their ideals of human perfection. For them the "beautiful people" are the socially and politically powerful and the ritually clean, that is, those who do all external things correctly.

Living Christ's Mission

"What good is it," declares St James, "if you say you have faith but do not have works?" (James 2:14). "I appeal to you," exhorts St Paul, "Do not be conformed to this world, but be transformed . . . so that you may discern . . . what is good and acceptable and perfect" (Rom 12:1, 2). What is good and acceptable is to live the mission of Christ in the world as he wishes. Jesus sought to describe how his followers must live his mission. There are six parables in Luke's Gospel which are stories of social, economic, and political reversal that should model how his faith-filled followers should behave:

- The Samaritan is good, not the status-proud priests and Levites (Luke 10: 30-37).
- Lazarus is good, not the wealthy rich man (Luke 16:19-31).
- The tax-collector is good, not the Pharisee (Luke 18:10-14).
- The last-seated at the wedding are good, not the rich invited ones (Luke 14:15-24).
- The prodigal son is good, not the envious and self-righteous brother (Luke 15:11-32).

In the Beatitudes he also describes what this mission must entail. Jesus speaks of two groups of people. First, the *anawim*. Their attitudes and lifestyles are contrary to the culture surrounding them. For them wealth, power, and selfishness have nothing to do with one's true happiness, which is only to be found in the reign of God and in his righteousness. The second are those advocates who protect the rights of the powerless and, suppressing self-love and ambition, show mercy. They struggle to develop peace in an unjust society, and are prepared to suffer for the defence of justice: "the kingdom of God is theirs" (Matt 5:3). In contrast to Matthew's version, in which the "poor" are referred to metaphorically, in Luke's text Jesus speaks of the materially poor. The lack of money is not praised or people are not condemned for having it. The expressions "rich" and "poor" are correlative; what the Beatitudes address is the gap between the two. Jesus is simply saying more bluntly than in Matthew's text that this chasm cannot be justified, and in the reign of God, there will be an economical reversal.

In the last speech of Jesus (Matt 25:31-46), prior to his passion, he unambiguously says that the ultimate indication of our effective commitment to his mission is whether or not we are being just to the powerless, the hungry, the oppressed, and the deprived in society. One's sentence on the day of judgement will be decided by one's attitudes and behaviour in this life. Jesus so identifies with the poor that when people refuse them justice they are refusing *him*, even if they are unconscious of this fact (Matt 25:40, 45).

Summary Points

- Myths are at the heart of every culture. emotionally embedded in them are a culture's fundamental values and assumptions about life. They claim to reveal in an imaginative and symbolic way fundamental truths about the world and human life;[109] *they are efforts to explain what usually is beyond empirical observation.* Myths are never intended to be science.
- Magic claims to control the uncontrollable through rituals that rest on empirically untested beliefs. Magical thinking and conspiracy theorizing belong to *mythos* and give meaning to their believers. *Mythos* seeks to articulate what cannot be stated in simple logical language. That is, myth does not attempt to be scientifically "factual" or rational, and so it cannot be demonstrated or verified.
- Unlike truths in *logos* the sole criterion for truths in mythologies is that people believe them. Conspiracy theories and magic are mythologically connected for two reasons: they both demand *belief* from their followers and both assume mystical manipulators behind the scenes.
- Magical rituals, including conspiracy theorizing, are rites of passage by which people believe they can safely transit from situations of no control to one of control.
- People become ritual leaders on their own authority or are assigned this task by others because it is assumed they have special knowledge to do so.
- The magical qualities of conspiracy theories in premodern cultures tend to be overt; in postmodern cultures, they are more commonly covert.
- The Bible never states that magic such as sorcery or witchcraft is fake but affirms that it is helpless against the power of God.[110] Magical thinking and actions are ultimate evils because they dare to substitute God with demons.

Discussion Questions

1 Explain to a friend why conspiracy thinking is a form of magical thinking.
2 Ponder the two versions of the Sermon on the Mount, the Beatitudes (Luke 6:20-26; Matt 5:3-12). What do you feel when you read them? Why are the Beatitudes termed the Charter for Christian living?

Notes

1 Francis Young, *Magic in Merlin's Realm: A History of Occult Politics in Britain* (Cambridge: Cambridge University Press, 2022), 327.
2 Susan Green, "A Spectrum of Magical Consciousness: Conspiracy Theories and the Stories We Tell Ourselves," *Anthropology Today*, vol. 38, no. 1 (2022): 1.
3 Michael Barkun, "Conspiracy Theories and the Occult," ed. Christopher Partridge, *The Occult World* (London: Routledge, 2016), 701.
4 For example, see Susan Greenwood, *The Anthropology of Magic* (London: Bloomsbury, 2009), 2–3; Susan Greenwood and Erik D. Goodwyn, *Magical Consciousness: An Anthropological and Neurobiological Approach* (New York: Routledge, 2016); Young, *Magic in Merlin's Realm*, 326–44; Gary Lackman, *Politics and the Occult The Left, The Right, and the Politically Correct* (Wheaton, IL: Quest Books, 2008); Roy Willis, "Magic," eds. Alan Barnard and Jonathan, *Encyclopedia of Social Anthropology* (London: Routledge, 1996), 342; Birgit Meyer and Peter Pels, eds., *Magic and Modernity: Interfaces of Revelation and Concealment* (Stanford: Stanford University Press, 2003); Henrietta L. Moore and Todd Sanders, eds., *Magical Interpretations, Material Realities: Modernity, Witchcraft and the Occult in Postcolonial Africa* (London: Routledge, 2001).
5 See S.F. Nadel, "Witchcraft in Four African Societies: An Essay in Comparison," *American Anthropologist*, vol. 54, no. 1 (2009): 18–29.
6 See Meredith McGuire, *Religion: The Social Context* (Belmont, CA: Wadsworth, 1997), 115; David S. Katz, *The Occult Tradition: From the Renaissance to the Present Day* (London: Pimlico, 2007), 1–2.
7 McGuire, *Religion*, 115.
8 See Charlotte Seymour-Smith, "Magic," *Macmillan Dictionary of Anthropology* (London: Macmillan Press, 1986), 175.
9 See Edmund R. Leach, "Magic," eds. Julius Gould and William L. Kolb, *A Dictionary of the Social Sciences* (London: Tavistock Publications, 1964), 398.
10 See *The New Collins Dictionary and Thesaurus*, ed. William T. McLeod (London: Collins, 1987), 1008.
11 See Alfred Kroeber and Clyde Kluckhohn, *Culture: A Critical Review of Concepts and Definitions.* Papers of the Peabody Museum

of American Archaeology and Ethnology 47, no. 1 (Cambridge: Harvard University Press, 1952), 5.
12 Edward Tylor, *Primitive Culture*, Vol. 1 (New York: Harper, 1871), 1.
13 See Alan Barnard, *History and Theory in Anthropology* (Cambridge: Cambridge University Press, 2000), 158–84; Kathryn Tanner, *Theories of Culture: A New Agenda for Theology* (Cambridge: Cambridge University Press, 1997), 3–58.
14 See James A. Beckford, *New Religious Movements and Rapid Social Change* (London: Sage, 1992), 19.
15 See Sheila G. Daveney, "Theology and the Turn to Cultural Analysis," eds. Delwin Brown, Sheila G. Davaney and Kathryn Tanner, *Converging on Culture: Theologians in Dialogue With Cultural Analysis and Criticism* (Oxford: Oxford University Press, 2001), 5.
16 See Anthony Giddens, *The Consequences of Modernity* (Stanford: Stanford University Press, 1990), 64.
17 Gerald A. Arbuckle, *Culture, Inculturation, and Theologians: A Postmodern Critique* (Collegeville, MN: Liturgical Press, 2010), 17. Italics in original.
18 For in-depth description, see Peter Brooker, *A Concise Glossary of Cultural Theory* (London: Arnold, 1999), 208–9.
19 Erich Fromm, *The Fear of Freedom* (London: Routledge & Kegan Paul, 1960), 240.
20 See Karen Armstrong, *Sacred Nature: How We Can Recover Our Bond With the Natural World* (London: The Bodley Head, 2022), 21–30; Gerald A. Arbuckle, *Fundamentalism at Home and Abroad: Analysis and Pastoral Responses* (Collegeville, MD: Liturgical Press, 2017), 31–2.
21 Rollo May, *The Cry for Myth* (New York: Delta, 1991), 26.
22 See Todd Sanders and Harry G. West, "Power Revealed and Concealed in the New World Order," eds. Harry G. West and Todd Sanders, *Transparency and Conspiracy: Ethnographies of Suspicion in the New World Order* (Durham/London: Duke University Press, 2003), 7–9.
23 See John Micklethwait and Adrian Wooldridge, *God Is Back: How the Global Rise of Faith Is Changing the World* (London: Penguin Books, 2009) and Monica D. Toft, Daniel Philpott, and Timothy S. Shah, *God's Century: Resurgent Religion and Global Politics* (New York: W.W. Norton, 2011).
24 See Gerald A. Arbuckle, *Earthing the Gospel: An Inculturation Handbook for the Pastoral Worker* (Maryknoll, NY: Orbis Books, 1990), 34–43.
25 Peter Berger, *Pyramids of Sacrifice: Political Ethics and Social Change* (Harmondsworth: Penguin, 1974), 32.
26 See Jenny Stewart, *Public Policy Values* (Basingstoke: Palgrave Macmillan, 2009), 192.
27 See Thomas Fawcett, *The Symbolic Language of Religion* (London: SCM Press, 1970), 101.

28 See Percy S. Cohen, "Theories of Myth," *Man: Journal of the Anthropological Institute*, vol. 4, no. 3 (1969): 337–53; William G. Dotty, *Mythography: The Study of Myths and Rituals* (Montgomery: University of Alabama Press, 1986), 41–71.
29 See Arbuckle, *Culture, Inculturation*, 19–42.
30 See description by Sam Keen, "The Stories We Live By," *Psychology Today* (December, 1988), 10; Clifford Geertz, *The Interpretation of Cultures* (London: Fontana Press, 1973), 216–18.
31 See Karen Armstrong, *The Battle for God: Fundamentalism in Judaism, Christianity, and Islam* (London: HarperCollins, 2001), 365.
32 May, *The Cry*, 26; see Greenwood, *The Anthropology of Magic*, 76–90.
33 See Marcel Mauss, *A General Theory of Magic*, trans. Robert Brain (London: Routledge and Kegan Paul, 1972); Roger Keesing, *Kwaio Religion* (New York: Columbia University Press, 1982), 50–6.
34 See John B. Haviland, *Gossip, Reputation, and Knowledge in Zinacantan* (Chicago: University of Chicago Press, 1977).
35 "Witch? Murderous Superstition in India," *The Economist* (October 21, 2017), 28.
36 See Kathleen A. Feeley, "Gossip as News: On Modern U.S. Celebrity Culture and Journalism, 1880–1960," *History Compass*, vol. 10, no. 6 (2012): 468.
37 See Robert Bocock, *Ritual in Industrial Society: A Sociological Analysis of Ritualism in Modern England* (London: George Allen and Unwin, 1974), 35–59; David I. Kertzer, *Ritual, Politics, and Power* (New Haven, CT: Yale University Press, 1988), 8–12; Roy A. Rappaport, *Ritual and Religion in the Making of Humanity* (Cambridge: Cambridge University Press, 1999), 107–38; Arbuckle, *Culture, Inculturation*, 81–98; Ronald L. Grimes, *The Craft of Ritual Studies* (New York: Oxford University Press, 2014), 165–210; Barry Stephenson, *Ritual* (Oxford: Oxford University Press, 2015), 70–101.
38 Bobby C. Alexander, "Ritual and Current Studies of Ritual: Overview," ed. Stephen D. Glazier, *Anthropology of Religion* (Westport: Greenwood Press, 1997), 139.
39 See Arnold Van Gennep, *The Rites of Passage*, trans. Monika Vizedom and Gabrielle Caffee (Chicago: University of Chicago Press, 1960).
40 See Gerald A. Arbuckle, *The Pandemic and the People of God: Cultural Impacts and Pastoral Responses* (Maryknoll, NY: Orbis Books, 2021), xii–xxiv, 39–74.
41 See Tom F. Driver, *The Magic of Ritual: Our Need for Liberating Rites That Transform Our Lives and Our Communities* (New York: HarperSanFrancisco, 1991), 93–4.

42 Joseph Campbell, *The Hero With a Thousand Faces* (Princeton, NJ: Princeton University Press, 1949), 30.
43 For example, Robert North comments: "Abraham is second only to Moses among New Testament mentions of biblical heroes." "Abraham," eds. Bruce M. Metzger and Michael D. Coogan, *The Oxford Companion to the Bible* (New York: Oxford University Press, 1993), 5; for 'hero' Abraham's role as a contemporary ritual leader of faith formation, rightly understood, see Jana M. Bennett, "On Pilgrimage With Abraham: How a Patriarch Leads Us in Formation of Faith," *Journal of Moral Theology*, vol. 1, no. 1 (2021): 20–39.
44 See S.F. Nadel, "Witchcraft in Four African Societies: An Essay in Comparison," *American Anthropologist*, vol. 54, no. 1 (2009): 18–29; Norman Cohn, "The Myth of Satan and His Human Servants," ed. Mary Douglas, *Witchcraft Confessions and Accusations*, (London: Tavistock, 1970), 3–16.
45 For example, see Kerry Prendeville, *The Ghari Story: Footprints in Sand and Time* (Auckland: Signature Press, 2021), 101–24.
46 See Leonard B. Glick, "Sorcery and Witchcraft," ed. Peter Ryan, *Encyclopedia of Papua and New Guinea*, vol. 2 (Carlton, Vic: Melbourne University Press, 1972), 1080–2.
47 See Pamela J. Stewart and Andrew Strathern, *Witchcraft, Sorcery, Rumors, and Gossip* (Cambridge: Cambridge University Press, 2004).
48 Clyde Kluckhohn noted that the fear of being accused a witch among the Navaho people can serve as an economic leveling mechanism: "A rich man knows that if he is stingy with his relatives or fails to dispense generous hospitality . . . he is likely to be spoken of a witch." *Navaho Witchcraft* (Boston: Beacon Press, 1944), 111; see also Monica Wilson, *Communal Rituals of the Nyakyusa* (London: Oxford University Press, 1959); Lucy Mair, *Witchcraft* (London: Weidenfeld and Nicolson, 1969).
49 See Victor Turner, *The Drums of Affliction: A Study of Religious Processes Among the Ndembu of Zambia* (Ithaca, NY: Cornell University Press, 1968), 46–51. Among the Kainantu, the Kuma, and the Orokaiva peoples in Papua New Guinea sorcery accusations act both as an important medium for expressing enmity and as an excuse for initiating warfare. See Peter Lawrence and M.J. Meggitt, "Introduction," eds. Peter Lawrence and Mervin J. Meggitt, *Gods, Ghosts and Men in Melanesia* (Melbourne: Oxford University Press, 1965), 8.
50 See Norman Cohn, *Europe's Inner Demons: An Enquiry Into the Great Witch Hunt* (London: Sussex University Press & Heinemann, 1975); "Why Connecticut Is Exonerating Witches," *The Economist* (March 2, 2023), 15.
51 "Witch? Murderous Superstition in India," *The Economist* (October 21, 2017), 28.
52 McGuire, *Religion: The Social Context*, 134.

53 See Garry W. Trompf, *Payback: The Logic of Retribution in Melanesian Religions* (Cambridge: Cambridge University Press, 1994), 143–4.
54 Trompf, *Payback*, 363.
55 See Janice Reid, *Sorcerers and Healing Spirits* (Sydney: Australian National University Press, 1983), 152.
56 See Edward E. Evans-Pritchard, *Witchcraft, Oracles and Magic Among the Azande* (Oxford: Clarendon Press, 1937); Timothy Larsen, *The Slain God: Anthropologists and the Christian Faith* (Oxford: Oxford University Press, 2014), 80–119.
57 For an example see Peter Lawrence, *Road Belong Cargo: A Study of the Cargo Movement in the Southern Madang District New Guinea* (Manchester: Manchester University Press, 1964); Kenneth Burridge, *Mambu: A Study of Melanesian Cargo Movements and Their Social and Ideological Background* (London: Methuen 1960).
58 See Peter Buck, *The Coming of the Maori* (Wellington: Whitcombe and Tombs, 1958), 404–13.
59 Joan Metge, *The Maoris of New Zealand* (London: Routledge & Kegan Paul, 1976), 92.
60 Metge, *The Maoris*, 92.
61 See Ineke M. Lazar, "*Ma'I Aitu:* Culture-Bound Illnesses in a Samoan Migrant Community," *Oceania*, vol. 55, no. 3 (1985): 161–81.
62 See Richard A. Goodman, "Some *Aitu* Beliefs of Modern Samoans," *The Journal of the Polynesian Society*, vol. 80, no. 4 (1971): 463–79.
63 For analyses of witch doctors and health, see E. Fuller Torrey, *Witchdoctors and Psychiatrists: The Common Roots of Psychology and Its Future* (New York: Harper & Row, 1972); Susan Fernando, *Mental Health, Race and Culture* (London: Macmillan, 1991), 150, 166.
64 See Lucy Mair, *Witchcraft* (New York: McGraw Hill, 1969), 76–101.
65 Evans-Pritchard, *Witchcraft, Oracles*, 337–8. Italics not in original.
66 See Arthur Kleinman, *Patients and Healers in the Context of Culture: An Exploration of the Borderland Between Anthropology, Medicine, and Psychiatry* (Berkeley: University of California Press, 1980), 203–58.
67 Charlotte Seymour-Smith, *Macmillan Dictionary of Anthropology* (London: Macmillan, 1986), 256; see "Shamanism Is Britain's Fastest Growing Religion: Climate Anxiety Helps to Explain Its Rising Popularity," *The Economist* (February 9, 2023) (PDF).
68 Francis Young, *Magic in Merlin's Realm: A History of Occult Politics in Britain* (Cambridge: Cambridge University Press, 2022), 330–1. See Gary Lachman, *Politics and the Occult: The Left, the Right, and the Radically Unseen* (Wheaton, IL: Quest Books, 2008), 233–9, and *Dark Star Rising: Magick and Power in the Age of Trump* (New York: Penguin Random House, 2018), ix–xxii, 1–102.
69 See Gerald A. Arbuckle, *Violence, Society, and the Church: A Cultural Approach* (Collegeville, MN: Liturgical Press, 2004), 101–24.

70 See Owen Davies, *A Supernatural War: Divination and Faith During the First World War* (Oxford: Oxford University Press, 2018), 218–32.
71 Niall Ferguson, *Doom: The Politics of Catastrophe* (London: Allen Lane, 2021), 64. Italics not in original; see Eugene Subbotsky, "The Belief in Magic in the Age of Science," *SAGE Open* (January–March, 2014): 1–17.
72 Andrew Greeley, "Magic in the Age of Faith," *America* (October 9, 1993), 14.
73 See McGuire, *Religion*, 114. It is claimed that Nancy Reagan, the wife of president Ronald Reagan, and Princess Diana consulted astrologers. See Greenwood, *The Anthropology of Magic*, 3.
74 See McGuire, *Religion*, 116–17.
75 Francis Young, *Magic in Merlin's Realm: A History of Occult Politics in Britain* (Cambridge: Cambridge University Press, 2022), 330.
76 Young, *Magic in Merlin's*, 327.
77 Eric Kurlander, *Hitler's Monsters: A Supernatural History of the Third Reich* (New Haven: Yale University Press, 2017), 299–300; see also Nicholas Goodrick-Clarke, *Occult Roots of Nazism: Secret Aryan Cults and Their Influence on Nazi Ideology* (New York: New York University Press, 1985). He argues that Nazism was influenced by powerful millenarian and occult sects that thrived in Germany and Austria fifty years before the rise of Hitler.
78 See Birgit Meyer and Peter Pels, eds., *Magic and Modernity: Interfaces of Revelation and Concealment* (Stanford: Stanford University Press, 2003).
79 See Peter Geschiere, *On Witch-Doctors and Spin-Doctors: The Role of "Experts" in Africa and American Politics* (Stanford: Stanford University, 2003); Green, *The Anthropology of Magic*, 3.
80 See Dan Stone, "Nazism as Modern Magic: Bronislaw Malinowski's Political Anthropology," *History and Anthropology*, no. 14 (2003): 203–18.
81 Alfred Rosenberg, cited by Kurlander, *Hitler's Monsters*, ix.
82 SS, an abbreviation of Schutzstaffel, was Hitler's elite military corps.
83 See Michael Polanyi, *Personal Knowledge: Towards a Post-Critical Philosophy* (Chicago: University of Chicago Press, 1958), 287–92; Erica Lagalisse, *Occult Features of Anarchism* (Oakland, CA: PM Press, 2019), 64–9.
84 See Ted Morgan, *Reds: McCarthyism in Twentieth-Century America* (New York: Random House, 2003).
85 See Susan Greenwood, "A Spectrum of Magical Consciousness: Conspiracy Theories and the Stories we Tell Ourselves," *Anthropology Today*, vol. 38, no. 1 (2022): 1; "QAnon and Other Delusions," *The Economist* (January 30, 2021), 32.
86 Greenwood, "A Spectrum of Magical Consciousness," 4. In a survey published in early 2022, "The Persistence of QAnon in the Post-Trump Era: An Analysis of Who Believes the Conspiracies," 25%

Republicans compared to 9% Democrats are QAnon believers. PRRI (February 24, 2022), Washington, DC. (PDF)
87 See Roger Griffin, *Fascism* (Oxford: Oxford University Press, 1995), 3.
88 See David Potter, *Disruption: Why Change Things?* (Oxford: Oxford University Press, 2021), 276–7.
89 Francis Young, *Magic in Merlin's Realm*, 330.
90 See Melissa Etehad, "Pencil or Pen? An Unusual Conspiracy Theory Grips Brexit Vote," *The Washington Post* (June 23, 2016), (PDF); Edwin Coomasaru, "Magical Thinking: Is Brexit an Occult Phenomenon?" *The Irish Times* (February 18, 2019) (PDF); Amy Davidson Sorkin, "The Magical Thinking around Brexit," *The New Yorker* (March 25, 2019) (PDF); Daniel Jolley, Karen M. Douglas, Marta Marchlewska, Aleksandra Cichocka, and Robbie Sutton, "Examining the Links between Conspiracy Beliefs and the EU 'Brexit' Referendum Vote in the UK: Evidence from a Two-Wave Survey," *Journal of Applied Social Psychology*, vol. 52, no. 2 (2021) (PDF).
91 "Britain and the EU: The End of Magical Thinking," *The Economist* (January 7, 2023), 8.
92 "Politics: The After-Party, *The Economist* (October 7, 2023), 46–7.
93 See Arbuckle, *Violence, Society*, 170–1.
94 See Michael Pusey, *Economic Rationalism in Canberra: A Nation Building State Changes Its Mind* (Cambridge: Cambridge University Press, 1992), 59–75.
95 See David C. Korten, *When Corporations Rule the World* (London: Earthscan, 1996), 103.
96 Noam Chomsky defines neoliberalism as "an ideology devoted to establishing more firmly a society based on the principle of private affluence, public squalor," *The Precipice: Neoliberalism, the Pandemic and the Urgent Need for Radical Reform* (London: Penguin, 2021), 122; see also critique of neoliberalism by Martin Wolf, *The Crisis of Democratic Capitalism* (New York: Penguin Press, 2023), 83–117.
97 Nancy Isenberg comments: "The former Speaker of the House [of Representatives] John Boehner (2011–2015) publicly equated joblessness with personal laziness." *White Trash: The 400-Year Untold History of Class in America* (New York: Penguin, 2016), 319.
98 John Micklethwait and Adrian Woolridge, *The Witch Doctors: What Management Gurus Are Saying, Why It Matters and How to Make Sense of It* (London: Heinemann, 1996), 15; see Gary Gerstle, *The Rise and Fall of the Neoliberal Order* (Oxford: Oxford University Press, 2022) and Craig Calhoun, Dilip Parameshwar Gaonkar, and Charles Taylor, *Degeneration of Democracy* (Cambridge: Harvard University Press, 2022).
99 Pope Francis, Encyclical Letter *Fratelli Tutti* (On the Fraternity and Social Friendship) (Vatican: October 3, 2020), par. 168. Italics not in original.
100 Pope Francis, Apostolic Exhortation *Evangelii Gaudium* (The Joy of the Gospel) (Vatican: 2015), par. 53.

101 See Arbuckle, *Fundamentalism*, 77–81; Wolf, *The Crisis of Democratic Capitalism*, 208–14.
102 Paul Collins, *The Future of Capitalism* (London: Penguin Books, 2019), 4,5. Collins is Professor of Economics and Public Policy, Oxford University.
103 David Hume cited by Micklethwait and Woolridge, *The Witch Doctors*, 15.
104 See John L. McKenzie, *Dictionary of the Bible* (London: Geoffrey Chapman, 1965), 536.
105 See Drorah O'Donnell Setel, "Witch," eds. Bruce M. Metzger and Michael D. Coogan, *The Oxford Companion to the Bible* (Oxford: Oxford University Press, 1993), 805.
106 See also Exod 22:17; Lev 19:31; 20:27.
107 See Ronald E. Clemens, "The Book of Deuteronomy," *The New Interpreter's Bible Vol 2* (Nashville, TN: Abington Press, 1998), 428–9.
108 See Jerome H. Neyrey, "Bewitched in Galatia: Paul and Cultural Anthropology," *The Catholic Biblical Quarterly*, vol. 50, no. 1 (1988): 72–100.
109 See Arbuckle, *Earthing the Gospel*, 26–43, and *Culture, Inculturation*, 19–42.
110 See John L. McKenzie, *Dictionary of the Bible* (London: Geoffrey Chapman, 1965), 536.

Conclusion

When I was a young student in Rome in 1959, I was visited by a desperately homesick, Australian friend. Everything in Italy confused him. The speed of the traffic frightened him. To make matters worse, they drove on the wrong side of the road! He felt totally lost. Nothing Italian appealed to him. He was in the chaos of profound culture shock; that is a reaction that is blind and irrational, a subconscious escape from a culturally different and disagreeable environment. To distract him I took him on a walk in the countryside. Suddenly he ran ahead of me. Why? Well, he saw on the roadside an Australian blue gum tree. He tearfully hugged it. At last he felt the comfort of something normal and familiar from home. With that, his culture shock began to leave him and I could help him to understand his nonsensical reactions to a different cultural setting.

However, nations, not just individuals, can suffer the chaos of profound cultural shock. The recent pandemic caused a massive global culture shock to nations and millions of people. Securities were suddenly undermined. Nothing seemed normal again. Covid-19 may have weakened, but no single crisis since the Second World War has left so many nations stunned by its ongoing cultural, economic, and political consequences. When big spectacular cultural disruptions happen, such as the pandemic, the political, social, and economic consequences take years, even generations, to play out. And they spin in unpredictable directions, such as we globally see now. People are prone to grasp anything, including irrational conspiracy theories, scapegoating, and magic that makes sense of what is happening (Chapters 2–4).

Internationally, there is a surge of nationalism and racism. Nationalisms and economic crises are socially dangerous mixes. Memories of the outcome of the Great Depression and nationalisms of the 1930s give reality to our fears. Existing nationalistic divisions between groups are widening and hardening. What have been skirmishes in the past are now turning into violent warfare. The rising tide of nationalism is turning the long-simmering discontent in both rich and poor countries into support for populism, particularly when adeptly fostered by autocratic politicians such as Donald Trump in America, or Recep Tayyip Erdogan in Turkey. They are supported by widespread disinformation and conspiracy theories. When their followers finally grasp that the groundless conspiracy promises fail to be realized, the trauma for individuals and their cultures intensifies.

The Western system of government is based on democratic values. Now we cannot any longer take these values for granted. Globally, democracy and human rights are in retreat. The number of democracies has been lessening under the influence of autocratic leaders. Even well-established democracies are now threatened in ways that few imagined possible a short time ago. Why is this so? Why have so many citizens in the Western world, despite years of education, become susceptible to the enticements of irrational conspiracy theories? Martin Wolf claims this is due to the loss of democratic citizenship. Western democracy has become decoupled from the duties of citizenship. People have been exhorted to exercise democratic power while being released from the obligation to make sacrifices for the benefit of others.[1] Likewise David Brooks writes that Americans

> inhabit a society in which people are no longer trained in how to treat others with kindness and consideration. Our society has become one in which people feel licensed to give their selfishness free rein. . . . We live in a society that's terrible at moral formation. . . . A culture that leaves people morally naked and alone leaves them without the skills to be decent to one another.[2]

This is why the many lessons in the biblical parable of the Good Samaritan are so crucial in forming people to be ethically good citizens and less prone to the dangerous attractions of conspiracy theorizing, scapegoating, and magic. In the story a racially despised Samaritan man goes to the aid of a traveller beaten and left half-dead by bandits (see Chapter 3). It is a story that still serves, even in contemporary secular society, as a reference point for measuring policy options including the ethical formation of citizens. At the heart of this story are the values of truth, respect for human rights, solidarity with the marginalized, equity, compassion, mercy, and social justice. There are three people other than the severely injured Jew: a priest, a Levite, and the Samaritan. The parable ends with this question from the narrator to the lawyer who had originally asked the question about who is his neighbour: "Which of these three, do you think, was the neighbour to the man who fell into the hands of the robbers?" (Luke 10:36) The lawyer replies: "The one who showed mercy." Then "Jesus said to him, 'Go and do likewise'" (Luke 10: 37).

Chaos can be a blessing! Surprised? Not if we read the Scriptures and find that chaos in its many synonyms is a dominant theme in both the Old

Testament and the New Testament. The Israelite prophets and the psalmists often use the imagery of chaos in order to highlight the opposite, namely, the ongoing inventive and redemptive action of God.[3] God's face is suddenly hidden, throwing the Israelites into a state of despair (Ps 30: 7). Then through God's compassionate action they discover new life in their experience of the chaos: "You have turned my mourning into dancing; you have taken off my sackcloth and clothed me with joy" (v.11). In the time of St Paul when devotees of the scriptures were confronted with social and political chaos around them, he wrote to console them:

> We know that the whole creation has been groaning in labor pains until now; and not only the creation, but we ourselves, who have the first fruits of the Spirit, groan inwardly while we wait for adoption, the redemption of our bodies. For in hope we were saved. . . . Likewise the Spirit helps us in our weakness; for we do not know how to pray as we ought, but that very Spirit intercedes with the sighs too deep for words. And God, who searches the heart, knows what is the mind of the Spirit, because the Spirit intercedes for the saints according to the will of God.
>
> (Rom 8:22-27)

Using the analogy of a woman giving birth, St Paul describes the whole of creation, humanity, ourselves, struggling perilously forward with groans and travails, yearning for the final transformation. We are already sharing, however imperfectly, the transformed world born through the resurrection in Christ: "the sufferings of the present time are not worth comparing with the glory about to be revealed to us" (Rom 8:18). We are in the liminal stage of a rite of passage,[4] the in-between-time in which we have received "the first fruits" of our redemption as God's children, but its completeness has yet to be *fully* embraced. Then "Death will be no more; mourning and crying and pain will be no more, for the first things have passed away" (Rev 21:4) – "the new heavens and the new earth where righteousness is at home" (2 Pet 3:13).

This rite of passage is an enigmatic or paradoxical mixture – simultaneously a taste of the transcendence and an experience of belonging in the here and now. Hope keeps us moving forward on track. We are not lost. God is present in the midst of the pain. God, indeed, is groaning in labour also. The chaotic experience of the pandemic and its aftermath remind us that we are in midst of this rite of passage, and our ritual guide, and one with us, is the Spirit of Jesus. The Spirit of Jesus, our journey's companion, is *with* us, groaning *with* us, interceding *for* us;[5] it is a cooperative action of the praying Christian with the revitalizing encouragements of the Spirit.[6] Paul reminds Christians that a central task in this in-between-time is to pray, with the Spirit taking the lead as it were, in the midst of world's pains.[7] It is time for lamentation, for prayer, in the midst of the present chaotic times: "How long must I bear pain in the soul, and have sorrow in my heart all day long? Consider and answer me, O Lord my God! . . . But I trusted in your steadfast love; my heart shall rejoice in your salvation" (Ps 13:2,3,5). Lamentation is inspired by hope.[8]

Notes

1 See Martin Wolf, *The Crisis of Democratic Capitalism* (New York: Penguin Press, 2023), 312–44.
2 David Brooks, "How America Got Mean," *The Atlantic* (August 14, 2023) (PDF), 3,11; see Gerald A. Arbuckle, *The Pandemic and the People of God: Cultural Impacts and Pastoral Responses* (Maryknoll, NY: Orbis Books, 2021), 89–100; Michael Sandel comments the world of business "has become detached from morals and . . . we need somehow to reconnect them." Michael J. Sandel, *What Money Can't Buy: The Moral Limits of the Markets* (New York: Farrar, Straus and Giroux, 2012), 6.
3 Biblically, "chaos" and its many synonyms such as the "Pit", "grave", "wilderness", means a state of utter confusion and fear, totally lacking in organization or predictability; it is the antithesis of cosmos. Walter Brueggemann writes "that the Bible is much more preoccupied with the threat of chaos than it is with sin and guilt . . . The storm produces a more elemental, inchoate anxiety, a sense of helplessness . . . It is bottomless in size and beyond measure in force . . . .." *Inscribing the Text* (Minneapolis: Fortress Press, 2004), 51.
4 The "liminal" or "liminality", an anthropological expression, is the precarious stage in a journey of change when travellers have forsaken the past and strain forward to reach their journey's end inspired by an interiorized vision of the future.
5 This text does not support providentialism, that is, the belief that all events are controlled by God. Providentialists assert that the pandemic is retribution for sins. Earlier Revered Jerry Falwell interpreted the 9/11 attack on the World Trade Center, New York, as divine retribution for America's sins. See Michael J. Sandel, *The Tyranny of Merit: What's Become of the Common Good* (London: Allen Lane, 2020), 45. Providentialism is particularly popular among Evangelical Christians, but it has supporters among American Catholic groups. See Rebecca Bratten Weiss, "Covid-19 Pandemic Has Revealed a Dangerous Providentialism among Catholics," *National Catholic Reporter* (September 3, 2020), www.ncronline.org/news/opinion/covid-19-pandemic-has-revealed-dangerous-providentialism-among-catholics (Accessed September 22, 2020).
6 See Sarah Coakley, *God, Sexuality, and the Self: An Essay 'On the Trinity'* (Cambridge: Cambridge University Press, 2013), 112.
7 See Robert Jewett, *Romans: A Commentary* (Minneapolis: Fortress Press, 2007), 508–28.
8 See Arbuckle, *The Pandemic and the People of God*, xxiv–xxvii.

Index

1960s United States 35
2008 financial crisis 40, 64, 70, 104

aboriginal America: Shamanism in 97
aboriginals *see* Yolngu people
Abraham (biblical) 111n43
Adam (biblical) 4, 22, 85
AfD *see* Alternative for Germany Party
Africa: democracy threatened in 76; premodern cultures of 93; Shamanism in 97; *see also* Azande people; South Africa
African Americans: AIDS conspiracy regarding 34; Welch's claims regarding 35
AIDS conspiracy theory 34
Alternative for Germany Party (AfD) 69–70
alt-right 99
Ananias 47
Angeli, Juke 101
anti-Catholicism 34, 66–7; Americanness of 81n79
anti-communist conspiracy theorizing 100–1; *see also* McCarthyism
anti-democratic leaders 70, 72
anti-immigration: Brexit and 102; leaders 69; movements 66
anti-globalization nationalists 80n60
anti-Irish bigotry 66
anti-lockdown rally: New Zealand 1

anti-Muslim rhetoric 69
anti-Semitism 63, 67
anti-vaccine conspiracy theories 2
Antoun, Richard 66
Aquinas *see* St. Thomas Aquinas
Aryanism 3, 33, 48, 63
Asgard 101
Asia: Obama born in, claims regarding 10; Shamanism in 97; Trump's claims regarding 70; *see also* China
astrology and astrologers 98, 100, 113n73
atomic bomb 101
Australia: Yolngu peoples 95
Austria: Covid-19 lockdowns in 83n113; occult sects in 113n77; premodern cultures of 93
authoritarianism 42; populist 3, 68–9; fascist 102; religious 65; Trump 72, 103; Western regression towards 76
autocracy 65; current rise of 72–3, 76; nationalism and 116–17
autocrats 21
Azande people 95–7, 100

Balkans 72
Barkun, Michael 3, 34, 55, 86
Barley, S. R. 9
Barthes, Roland 14
Beatitudes 24–5, 105, 108n2
Beddoes, Zanny Minton 72
Belarus 72

Index 121

belief: conspiracy 33–4, 40–2; conspiracy theory and 48; magic and 87; magic and conspiracy thinking's demand for 3, 86, 90, 107; magical mythological thinking and 99; mythos and xiv; myths as 89; occult 100; questioning 44; unquestioned 93; untested 92, 107; untrue 45
Bergmann, Eirikur 37
Biden, Joe 43, 72
Birchers 34–5
Black people 10, 61, 95; "good" 71
black mass 36
"Blessed," meaning of 24–5
blindness: biblical story of man cured of 46; Christ's restoring of sight 106; Paul and Elymas 105
blind trust, i.e. trusting in someone blindly 42
Bolsonaro, Jair 32, 70
Book of Deuteronomy 4, 23, 75, 104
Book of Exodus 46, 73
Book of Leviticus 22
Book of Revelation 105
Brazil 32, 70, 72
Breivik, Anders Behring 43
Brexit 102–3; "Take Back Control" slogan 62
Brothers of Italy Party 70
brook, deceitful 9
Brooks, David 117
Brother Lawrence 11
Brueggemann, Walter 84n131, 119n3
Buber, Marin 14
Buhari, Muhammadu 32
bullets and bombs 66
bullying 7, 11, 13
Butter, Michael 41, 43

Campbell, Joseph 92
Canaan 22
Canada: belief in astrology in 98; Trump-like beliefs in 33
cancel culture 68
Capitol building, US, storming of 37, 41, 71, 86, 101; *see also* insurrection
Carlson, Tucker 37
Catholic theology 5n7
Catholics and Catholicism: anti-Catholicism 34, 66–7, 81n79; contemporary US 98
Chansley, Jacob 101
chaos: Bible's preoccupation with 119n3; Biblical meaning of 119n3; as blessing 117–18; conspiracy theories and 31, 44, 56; cultural 56; culture as protection from 20; cultures falling into 40; culture shock and 116; fascism as response to 102; fundamentalism as reaction to fear of 65; intensification of gossip in times of 19–20; numbness of 64; political xii, 48, 56; pure terror as 40, 63; ritual as means to manage 92; world of 3
charms (magical) 98
Chesterton, G. K. 97
Chick, Jack 36
Chile 102
China 33; Communist Party takeover of 101; Covid-19 and 39; emergency powers assumed by 72
Chomsky, Noam 114n96
Christ xiii, 24–5; belief in 46–7; body of 32; death of 31, 59; faith in 105; living Christ's mission 106–7; as Good Samaritan 75; passion of 107; revelation of 45, 48
Christendom 63
Christian nation, US as 34, 67
Christian premillennialism 1, 43; definition of 53n86
Christians 4; called to be truth-tellers 48; Catholics as not Christian, conspiracy theories regarding 36

Christian scriptures xii
civil right activism, US 14
civil rights movement, US 35
Civil War, US 67
Clement of Alexandria (church Father) 47
Clinton, Hillary 36–7
Cogley, John 81n79
Cohn, Roy 28n38
Collins, Louise 13
Collins, Paul 103–4
Comet Ping Pong Pizza 36
compassion xiv, 74, 76, 117
conspiracism, new 37–8; disinformation and 43; scapegoating 55
conspiracy theorizing: gossip and 2, 7–25; magical mythological thinking as form of 99; scapegoating and xiv–xv, 55–76
conspiracy theory 31–48; America First 35; deep state 37; defining 33–4, 48; flourishing of 40–2; fringe 37; global theories 36–8, 48; harm caused by 2–3, 42–3; local conspiracies 34–6, 48; magical thinking and xiv, 3–4, 86–108; overview of 1–4; responding to 44–5; Scriptural critique 4, 45–8; as term 49n1; Trump Experience case study of 38–40; types of 34–40
conspiracy without theory 37–8
conspiratorial style 42
conspiratorial thinking 37, 39
Cooper, Ed 21
Coughlin, Edward Charles 6–7
Covid-19: autocracy's rise during 72; care home resident deaths in England and Wales 72; conspiracy theories about 1, 43, 65–7; cultural trauma of 40; democracies threated by 65–7; disinformation and lies and 21; Holland lockdowns and rioting over 43; India's scapegoating of Muslims 43; infoepidemic 32; Johnson's poor handling of 71; pre-Covid-19 64–5; Putin's conspiracy theories about 32; shock of 64; Trump's conspiracy theories and lies about 33, 39
cowboy hero 40
cultural anthropology xii, 2
cultural chaos xiii; conspiracy theories' flourishing in times of 48
cultural codes 24
cultural crises 33; conspiracy theories as stories in times of 40–1, 91; exploitation of people during 43
cultural device: gossip used as 15
cultural disintegration 60
cultural essentialism 58
cultural norms 93
cultural prejudice: against Jews 10
cultural solidarity 62
cultural status quo 17, 20
cultural template: myths as 90
cultural trauma 63–4; 2008 Financial Disaster as example of 64; 1820s US as period of 66; 1830s US as period of 66; 1960s US as period of 35; conspiracy-fed nationalism and 76; Covid-19 as 65; Great Depression as example of 64; Lone Ranger myth as solution to 39–40; populist leaders feeding off 68; scapegoating intensified by 55–6, 63–5; *see also* Covid-19
cultural unconscious 9
cultural upheaval 2; gossip and 19
culture: American conservatives' concern and resentment regarding 70; "billiard ball" model of 88; 'cancel' 68; chaos and 20, 40; conspiracy theories and breakdown of 41–2; crumbling of security of 1; gossip as feature in 2, 7–10; ideology and 44; importance

of xii; Jewish 24; modern industrial 87; as *nomos* 20; non-literate 26n6; normality and 63; organizational 16; own versus other 75, 76; popular 34, 51n43; postmodern 86; postmodern definition of 88; premodern xiv, 86, 93, 99; "pure" 88; as purity system 62; racist 18; reception of Revelation and 48; shamans in 97; stories' importance to 40; subcultures 88; supernatural imaginary of 99; symbols, myths and rituals in 87–8, 90, 92, 107; toxic 14; traditional 17, 96; tribal 104; white people 37; Word of God in 47
culture of conspiracy 34
culture of walls 57
culture shock 116
culture unconscious 9–10

Danner, Mark 69
deep state 37, 68; American belief in 37
demagogue, demagogy 71–2, 83n115
democratic beacon, US s 72
democratic norms and values 35, 102, 117
Democratic Party, US 36–7
democracy: conspiratorial style as threat to 42; current crisis in 65, 76; delegitimization of 38; global retreat of 117; liberal 83n115; political leaders' rejecting 69–70; Trump's rejection of 70–2; US founding myth of 89; Western duties of citizenship decoupled from 117
demonization 3, 58, 71; of the poor 103
demons: metaphorical 23; substitution or replacing of God with xiv, 4, 86, 104, 107; summoning 91
denunciation 68

Desdemona (Shakespearean) 8
despotism 66, 83n115
Deuteronomic theology 104
Deuteronomy 4, 23, 75, 104
Diana (Princess of Wales) 113n73
disinformation 21, 43, 67–8, 117; Age of 20
divination 87, 98, 104
Douglas, Mary 58, 61–2
Douglas, Tom 57

Eisenhower, Dwight D. 35
Elkins, Caroline 62
Elymas 105
Enlightenment: denial of need for *mythos* 89, 97; fascism and 102; human perfectibility and 100
envy 16; accusation of sorcery and 96; gossip/gossips and 2, 7–8, 10–11, 14, 23; scapegoating and 56; Simon of Samaria and 105; St. Paul on (Discussion Question) 76
Erdogan, Recep Tayyip 69, 117
ethnocentrism 58–63; Kipling on 58; moral panic as type of 58; scapegoating and 76; tribal 63
ethno-medical beliefs 97
ethno-religious other 99
Evans, Hiram Wesley 67
Evans-Prichard, Edward 97, 100
Eve (biblical) 4, 22, 85
evil: ability to cause 92; collective 64; conspiracy theorists' perception of 44; conspiracy theorizing as xiv, 4; conspiracy theory as means to explain 48; gossip as 23–4; Jews as 63; magical thinking as 86, 104, 107; multiculturalism as 43; racism as 74; scapegoating as 55; transfer of evil to others 57; *see also* good and evil
evil deeds 73
"evil doers" 103
evil forces 34, 36; loss of the soul through 97; secret knowledge hidden by 99

evil intent 8, 22
"evil ones", stigmatization of 58
evil purpose 9
Exodus *see* Book of Exodus
Exodus, the 89
Eye of Horus 36
Ezekiel 104

faith: act of 33; bad 35; call to be open to truth 47–8; Christian 4, 47; in Christ the Redeemer 31, 45–6, 48, 105; dogmatic 44; Jesus' words on 46
faith imperative 105–6
Faithful Witness, Christ as 47
fake news 21, 39, 68
Falange (Spanish) 102
fascism 36, 72, 102; neo-fascism 99
fascists and fascist sympathizers in the US 71; Radical Agenda 83n111
Fauci, Anthony 32–3
Feltman, Charles 41
Ferguson, Niall 97
Fiji 18
Firth, Raymond xii
France: Covid-19 in 71; political fundamentalism in 80n60; rise of populism in 69
Francis (Pope) 5n5, 8, 55, 57, 65, 67, 103
Franklin, Benjamin 21
Freud, Sigmund and Freudian theory 9, 100
Fromm, Erich 88
fundamentalism: American 39, 67; blind or unquestioning trust as characteristic of 42; Catholic Church 67; Islamic 66; modern 66; myth of 71; National Union for Social Justice as example of 67; splitting theory and 60; terrorism and 43
fundamentalist: conspiracy theory 1; ideology 63; movement 65–6; as organized anger 66; slogans 80; thinking 45

Gash, D.C. 9
Geertz, Clifford 20
Germany 99–100; AfD party 69–70; Covid-19 lockdowns in 83n113; occult sects in 113n77; *see also* Aryanism; Hitler; Nazis and Nazism
Girard, Rene 58–9
Goebbels, Joseph 100
good and bad, separating 60
good and bad spirits 93
good and evil: battle between 2; knowing 22; struggle between 33
"Good" blacks and Indians 71
good faith effort 41
good health 93, 96
Goodhart, David 68
good news (biblical tidings of) 106
Good Samaritan parable xiv, 73–5, 117
good works, practice of 4
Gospels xii, 55; love and justice of 73; Luke 106; principles of nonviolence 59
gossip 7–25; defining 8–12; conspiracy theorizing and 2, 7–8; cultural upheaval and 19–21; malicious 8, 16, 23; power and 14–17; scriptural critique of 21–5; St. James on 25 (Discussion Question); violence and 12–13
gossips: shaming by 17–19
Grasso, Richard 28n38
grassroots reform 82n91
Great Replacement conspiracy theory 37
Greely, Andrew 98
Greene, Marjorie Taylor 37, 39
Green, Susan 86
green tea 18
Greenwood, Susan 101
grievance xiv, 68–70; populism and 76; Trump and politics of 69–70
Griffin, Roger 102

Guriev, Sergei 28n33
gypsies 63; *see also* Roma people

Hall, Edward 9–10
Hamas 66
Hammarskjold, Dag 15
Haring, Bernard 47
Hawley, Katherine 42
Herod 23–4, 47
Hess, Rudolf 100
Hezbollah 66
Himmler, Heinrich 100
Hitler, Adolf 56, 63, 100; anti-Semitic claims regarding Jews 3, 48, 49n14, 54n116, 63; censure of Jewish people 56; logic of racial pollution used by 63; Nazi obsession with the occult and 99–100; *see also* Aryanism
Hofstadter, Richard 38
Holland: Covid-19 lockdowns in 43
Hollenbach, David 75
Hollywood elite 36–7, 101
holy place 46
Holy Spirit 47–8
Hoover, J. Edgar 14, 28n38
Hume, David 104
Hungary 69
hungry: Jesus's message, "I was hungry" 75
hungry, the 107
Hunter, James 66
hunting *see* witch-hunting
hunting, language of 9

ideological conspiracy theorists, dialoguing with 44–5
ideological convictions 99
ideological extremism 2
ideological orientation, of fundamentalists 66
ideology 44–5; fundamentalist, of Hitler 63; neoliberalism as 114n96; populism as 67
I–It relationship 14
Illuminati 36–7, 50n27
infoepidemic 32

initiation rituals 91
insurrection and insurrectionists: domestic 71; US Capitol (January 6, 2021) 86, 101
intentionality 41
Iraneus (church Father) 47
Iraq 102
islanders: case study of gossip based on 15–16
Israel 24; ancient Judaism and 104; new, following the Exodus 89; prophets of 118; terrorist attack of 2023 on 66
Israelites 22, 46, 73–4; despair of 118

jealousy 10–12, 23, 56, 76
Jensen, Siv 69
Jeremiah (Biblical) 8–9
Jesus *see* Christ
Jewish culture: Jesus and 24
Jewish tradition 74
Jews 48; anti-Semitic conspiracy theorizing about 3, 33–4, 36–7, 48, 49n14, 54n116, 56, 63, 70, 99–100; conspiracy theories regarding the theft of the body of Christ and 32; Good Samaritan parable and 73; Great Replacement conspiracy theory about 37; persecution of 59, 63; racial inferiority of, Nazi-era claims regarding 99–100; Samaritan and priest at the well, story involving 117; Samaritan woman at the well and cultural prejudices against 10; scapegoating of 63
John (Biblical) 23
John Birch Society 34
John Paul I 42
John Paul II 48
Johnson, Boris 83n114, 83n115
Johnson, Mike 72
Jones, Alex 37
Joseph (Biblical) 8, 22–3
justice xiv; core value of 74; Jesus and 75, 107; love and, Gospels

of 73; parables as stories about 85n132; social 67, 117; suffering of poor in search of 106; as universal truth and value 76
Justin (church Father) 47

Kainantu people 111n49
Kennedy, John F.: assassination of 33–4, 36; conspiracy theories in American politics since 38; as traitor, accusation of being 35
Kennedy, Robert 14
King, Martin Luther, Jr. 74
Kipling, Rudyard 58
Klein, Melanie 60
Knight, Peter 34, 40
Know-Nothing Party, US 34, 67
Korean War 101
Ku Klux Klan 34, 67, 83n111
Kuma people 111n49
Kurlander, Eric 98–9

LaFrance, Adrienne 31, 62
Lazar, Ineke 96
Lazarus 56, 106
Le Pen, Marine 63, 69
Levites 106, 117
Lie, Trygve 14–15
Lincoln, Abraham 36
logos xiv, 3, 107; truth obtained via 86, 89–91, 107
Lone Ranger myth 39–40
Lukashenko, Alexander 72
Luke, Gospel of 106
Lyth, Isabel Menzies 58, 78n29

magic and magical thinking: conspiracy theorizing and xiv, 3–4; explaining 87–93; mythos and 86, 89–91; postmodernity and 97–104; premodernity and xiv, 93–7; Scriptural critique of 4, 104–7
magicians 105
magical mythological thinking, conspiracy theorizing as form of 99

Maori people 18, 96
Maori sickness (*mate Maori*) 96
marriage 69, 91
Marsden, Maori 18
Marshall, Chris 73–4
Marxian dialectical theory 100
Matthew (biblical) 106–7
May, Rollo 64
McCarthyism 100–1
McCarthy, Joseph 100–1; gossip used by 28n38; Republican backing of 43
McVeigh, Timothy 2
Meloni, Giorgia 70
melon plants 11
Merton, Klaus 10
Mescher, Marcus 74–5
Messiah 106
messianic leaders 95
Metge, Joan 96
Miller, Edward 42
misinformation *see* disinformation
Mjolnir 101
Modi, Narendra 32
moral consciousness 73
moral decay 67
morale 40–1
moral indignation 11, 39
moral order 61
moral panic 56, 58
Mounk, Yascha 64
Muirhead, Russell 37–8, 41, 61
murahachibu (silent ostracism) 17
Murphy, Vivek 21
Muslim ban, US (Trump) 39, 58
Muslims: America First racism and 35; Brevik's conspiracy theories about 43; conspiracy theories about 3, 69; Obama accused of being 37
Mussolini, Benito 102
mythical folklore 100
mythic core of fascism 102
mythlessness 64
mythological beliefs: civic 39
mythological sense of identity 44
mythology: Azande 96; cultural, need for leaders of magical

rituals to be imbued with 92–3; Enlightenment's denial of need for 89, 97; magical mythological thinking, conspiracy theorizing as form of 99; Marxist 100; neoliberal 103; Nordic 101; US's self-mythologizing 35, 38–9

mythos xiv, 3; magical thinking and 89–91, 107; truth obtained via 86, 89–91

myths xiv, 3; cultural 58; cultural solidarity and 62; culture and 87–9, 90, 107; fundamentalist 71; Genesis 4, 75; human experience and 91; paradigms distinct from 90; as "webs of significance" 40

nationalism: 1930s 65, 76; conspiracy-fed 76; Covid-19 and 65; extreme 60; racism and 116

National Policy Institute 83n111

National Security Agency (NSA) (US) 50

National Socialism 100; *see also* Nazis and Nazism

National Union for Social Justice (US) 67

nativism 99

Nazis and Nazism: conspiracy theorizing and new rise of 98; fascism and 102; Illuminati blamed for 36; magical thinking and 99–100; Muslims compared to 69; Neo-Nazi Ukrainians, conspiracy theories regarding 3, 13, 63; occult obsessions of 99–100

Nazi salute 83n111

negative partnership 62

neoliberalism 103–4

New Deal 67

New Testament: chaos as theme in 117–18; on conspiracy theorizing and magical thinking 105; Good Samaritan parable 73–5; on gossip 23–4; on magicians 105; Moses 111n43; scapegoating condemned by 55, 73; on truth-telling 47

New World Order 36

Nichols, Tom 72

North, Robert 111n43

Obama, Barack: conspiracy theories about 10, 37, 39

Obamacare 71

occult and occultism 3; conspiracy theories and 86; divination and 87; Nazism and 99–100; politics and 97–9

Old Testament xiii; on bearing false witness 46; chaos as theme in 117–18; on conspiracy theorizing and magical thinking 104, 105; honour and shame in 24; malicious gossip in 8, 22–3; scapegoating condemned by 55, 73; Serpent (Eden) as gossip 22

omens 98

Orban, Viktor 69

Orokaiva people 111n49

ostracism 17–18, 62

Othello (Shakespeare) 8

Packer, George 35

palmistry 98

Papua New Guinea 94–5, 111n49

Party for Freedom, the Netherlands 69

Paul the Apostle *see* St. Paul

paranoia iii, 1, 38; conspiratorial thinking and 37; Greene (MTG)'s harnessing of 39

paranoiacs: "clinical" 38; "political" 38

"paranoid political spokesman" 38

paranormal 100; *see also* occult

Parousia 47

Patterson, James 35

Pattinson, Stephen 18

Pharisees 19, 47, 55, 106

pharmaceutical industry 1
Pilate (Pontius) 44–5
Pinochet (General) 102
Pipes, Daniel 34
Pizzagate 36
Podesta, John 36
Polanyi, Michael 100
polluted, the 105
polluting behavior attributed to immigrants 35
pollution theory 61–3
Popper, Karl 49n1
populism 67–8; conspiracy theorizing and 55–76; nationalism and 116; right-wing 39
populist leaders 68–72; Bolsonaro 32, 70; Buhari 32; grievance embodied by xiv, 76; Johnson (Boris) 71; as leaders of magical rituals 92; Le Pen 63; Meloni 70; narcissism and 69; Putin 3; Trump 3, 38–9, 43, 69–71, 103; unscrupulous 43, 56; US Republicans in House and Senate 43
Populist Party, US 82n91
populist resentment 103
postmodern cultures 86, 88, 107
postmodernity 65; magic and conspiracy thinking in 97–104
premodern ancestors 89
premodern cultures 86
premodernity: examples of premodern conspiracy thinking 94–6; magic and conspiracy thinking in xiv, 93–7
prodigal son, parable of 12, 25 (Discussion Question), 106
Progress Party, Norway 69
projection 60
propaganda 13, 28, 32, 99
Propaganda Ministry, Nazi Germany 100
proportionality 41
Protestant America 66
Psalm 41 9

Psalm 64 9
Psalm 88 22
Psalm 119 4
psalmists 9, 13, 118
psalms: lamentation 46, 54n105
Putin, Vladimir 63; abuse of power facilitated by conspiracy theories 3; Covid-19 conspiracy theories spread by 32; media and gossip co-opted by 13; as "spin dictator" 28n33; Ukraine blamed for war by 72; Ukrainian Nazi conspiracy theories spread by 63
purity 47, 62; racial 63; social 94

QAnon 1, 36–7, 42; conspiracy theory 101; Republican believers versus Democrat believers, percentages of 114n86

racism 70, 74, 116; institutional 10, 75
Rahner, Karl 48
Rauch, Jonathan 43
Reagan, Nancy 113n73
Reagan, Ronald 113n73
revelation: divine 48; myth as medium of 90
Revelation, Book of *see* Book of Revelation
revelation of Jesus Christ 45, 48
revelation of God xii, 45
rites of passage 91–2, 118; liminal stage of 118
ritual: cultural 58, 62; culture and 87–9; initiative 91; lamentation psalms as 46; magic/magical 91–2, 107; meaning and 91–2; Mosaic 77n4; necessity of 92; neoliberalist 103; purpose of 92; secret 87, 95; transformative 91; Western 19
ritual leader: of magic rituals 92–3; McCarthy as 101

rituals of: curing 91; passage 91; voting for Brexit 102
ritual therapists, Samoan 96
Robertson, Pat 36
Romanticism 100
Roman ruler, Pontius Pilate as 44
Roma people 72
Roosevelt (President) 67
Rosenberg, Alfred 100
Rosenblum, Nancy 37–8
Rothschilds 37
rumour 14–15, 19; gossip distinct from 10

Saddam Hussein 102
Samoans 96
Sanhedrin Council 24
Sapphira 47
Satan 23, 46, 63
Satanism 36
scapegoating 55–77; of communists 34; conspiracism and 55; Covid-19 and threats to democracy 65–73; cultural chaos and 20; cultural trauma and 63–5; defining 56–7; divisions created by xiv, 3; envy and jealousy in 11; ethnocentrism and 58–63; Good Samaritan parable and 73–6; of Muslim minorities 43; origins of 57–8; Scriptural critique of 4, 73; shame and 56–7; strategic 57; us versus them framing applied in 33
Schwarzenegger, Arnold 40
September 11, 2001 66
Sermon on the Mount 108 (Discussion Question)
shamans and Shamanism 92, 96–7; QAnon Shaman 101
shame 4; honour and 24–5; used by gossipers 7, 17–19; scapegoating and 56–7
shamelessness, of Trump 69
Simon of Samaria 105
social defense 78n29

Solomon Islands 95
sorcery and sorcerers xiv, 44; Azande beliefs regarding 95; biblical views on 104–7; conspiracy theory and 94; fear of being accused of 93; Jews as "league of" 63; magical rituals and 91, 92; Maori beliefs regarding 96; New Testament views on 105–7; Old Testament views on 104; Samoa beliefs regarding 96; Tolai beliefs regarding 95; Yolngu beliefs regarding 95
Soros, George 37
South Africa 56
South America 76
Spacks, Patricia 13
spirits (supernatural) 91, 93; malignant 96
Spitzer, Eliot 28n38
splitting theory 60–1
Stallone, Sylvester 40
Starmer, Keir (Sir) 103
St. Benedict 21
St. James 23–4, 25 (Discussion Question), 106
St. John 23
St. John Paul II 48
St. Matthew 31
St. Paul 23, 76n2, 105–6
St. Peter 47, 105
St. Thomas Aquinas 18, 47
superstition 98, 104
Switzerland: Covid-19 lockdowns in 83n113

Taylor, Charles 73
Thor 101
Thunberg, Greta 32
Tolai people 95
treason 102
Treisman, Daniel 28n33
tribal cultures 104
tribal ethnocentrism 63, 76
tribalism 61–3
Trompf, Garry 95

Trump, Donald 69; abuse of power facilitated by conspiracy theories 3; America First of 35; authoritarianism of 72; Covid-19 and conspiracy theories by 1, 33, 56; grievance and 69; lying by 19; "Make America Great Again" 70; Muslim ban 58; narcissism of 69; Obama conspiracy theories spread by 10; populism of 70, 76; QAnon and 36–7; rigged election conspiracy theories spread by 38, 43; success of conspiracy theories spread by 43; xenophobia and white supremacy of 71
Trump Experience: case study 38–40
trust: in America, loss of 104; blind or unquestioning 42; breakdown of trust in government 35, 38, 41, 52n72; fear replacing 42; gossip as destroyer of 14–16; political, in the Balkans 72; Trump's undermining of 71
trustworthiness 47
truth: absolute 67; anthropological 40; bearing witness to 59; difficulty of dialoguing for 68; distortion of 44; faith and call to be open to 47–8; five foundational truths in Good Samaritan parable 74–5; *logos* and *mythos* 86, 89–90, 107; objective 35; unchanging 45; universal xiv; untruth iii; unverifiable xiii, 4
truthfulness 42
truth-telling: as Scriptural imperative 46–7

Van Gennep, Arnold 91
Vanguard America 83n111
Vatican 36
Vatican Press Office 42
Vanuatu 95
Voltaire 3

Welch, Robert 34–5
Western conspiracy, Putin's blaming of 32
Western consciousness, communism and 66
Western cultural tradition, story of Good Samaritan in 73
Western democracies: decoupling from duties of citizenship of 117; rise of extreme nationalism in 60
Westerns (film genre) 40
Western society 15, 19; fundamentalism in 66; magic and conspiracy theorizing in 86; *mythos* and 89; regression towards authoritarianism of 76; traumatic indigenous contact with 96
Whakamaa (shamed) 18
whispering campaigns xiii, 9, 23, 25
whites (white people) 10, 95; Great Replacement theory and 37; poor 61; working class and Trump 39
white supremacy 83n111; *see also* Ku Klux Klan
WHO *see* World Health Organization
wilderness 119n3
Wilders, Geert 69
witchcraft xiv, 91–5, 98; accusations of 91, 93; convinced believers in 44; gossip and 17; Scriptural critique of 104, 107
witches 92–7; malevolent 94
Witches Division, SS (Nazi) 100
witch-doctors 56, 92, 99; modern-day 103
witch-hunting 56, 63, 76; conspiracy thinking and 93–7; McCarthyism and 101

witch trials 100; New England 91
Wolf, Martin 83n115
women: Middle Ages conspiracy theories focused on 94; gossip and 12–13; scapegoating of 60; Trump's derogatory language towards 39; violence against 59–60
World Health Organization (WHO) 32

xenophobia 39, 70–1

Yahweh 73, 84n131
Yellowstone Wolf (Juke Angeli) 101
Yggdrasil 101
Yolngu tribe 95
Young, Francis 86, 97, 98, 102
Young, Jock 58

For Product Safety Concerns and Information please contact our EU
representative GPSR@taylorandfrancis.com
Taylor & Francis Verlag GmbH, Kaufingerstraße 24, 80331 München, Germany

www.ingramcontent.com/pod-product-compliance
Lightning Source LLC
Chambersburg PA
CBHW051751230426
43670CB00012B/2238